Sales, Swingers and Start-ups

Finding sales success in a start-up

Mark I LaRosa

Ordering Information

Quantity sales. Contact QuotaCrush at inquiries@quotacrush.com

Individual sales. Available thru local bookstores and online at Amazon.com

ISBN-978-0-615-96032-6

QuotaCrush Publishing

www.quotacrush.com

For nearly all my career, I've been involved in start-ups and helping them with their sales strategy. Be it as the founder, as the VP of Sales, board member, or as a consultant to the startup via my **QuotaCrush** practice, I've been helping entrepreneurs turn around their companies through sales. Most of them become profitable using the tactics and strategies contained in this book.

In most instances, the transition from "can't sell" to "selling" is very subtle – and is often about thinking about the product and the company the way a salesperson would – the way a prospect and customer would. Most of what I have done in my career is to help non-sales entrepreneurs understand the world of sales so that they can succeed. The other portion of what I have done is to help salespeople and entrepreneurs understand what selling is, and how to sell in and for a start-up. This is what I am hoping to bring across in this book.

I didn't start my career in sales. In fact, if you asked me when I was growing up if I'd ever consider being a salesman, I would have thought you were insane. Yet, looking back, I realize I was always a sales person. I loved talking to people and making deals, but since sales was not something you encouraged your kids to strive to do… I never really thought about it. In college, people jokingly called me "Senator LaRosa" because my deal making and gift of words was seen as something that would send me into politics, (and perhaps someday it will) but that wasn't what I saw as my path in life.

I was a software guy. I loved building software and tinkering on the PC. I got my first job at 13 years old building a computer system to handle all of the high schools computer needs from scheduling to grades to rank to attendance. Then, I started a consulting company to build custom computer systems for small companies and that carried me through college. Ten months after I graduated from Stevens Institute of Technology, I started a mobile software company.

I always knew that I was an entrepreneur at heart, but I still saw myself as the engineer – the software guy. Then, in my mobile start-up, I started going on lots of sales calls. I realized that all my work up to this point had actually trained me for sales, but I had a remarkably different perspective than most salespeople – I could talk tech. This meant that the CIO/CTO sale that I was trying… ACTUALLY WORKED! Why? I could understand their pain, their actual problems – and I could tell them EXACTLY how my solution would fix it. I could talk and design a deal on the fly that made tech people (my initial targets) comfortable.

About 2 years into building this company, I realized that I had hired some great technology people, and that I really loved selling the product and being in the field. I shut down the compiler that day and rarely returned. But, I had learned very important lessons about how to sell. I was able to get into the heads of the people to whom I was selling, because I had lived their lives. I had *felt their pain*, and it was that **empathy** that now drives every sales decision that I make – and my prospects appreciate it and turn into customers – often repeat, lifelong customers.

It has been my mission since then to help entrepreneurs understand sales – so that they can hire better, work better, and generate revenues for their companies. When a CEO understands what the sales function is, how salespeople think, how customers and prospects think, the entire process is better – and sales grow.

INTRODUCTION

Sales are the lifeblood of all organizations. There is not a business, non-profit, or organization in existence that does not have a sales function. It may be referred to as "strategic partnerships," "corporate advancement," "business development," or another alias, but the purpose remains the same. Sales transform a group of people with similar goals and ideas into a profitable organization capable of fulfilling a previously unmet need. It is the reason that all businesses exist – to serve an audience in some way.

Our society has grown weary of this fundamental function. The word "sales" carries a negative connotation – possibly as a result of ineffective, relentless telemarketers. Despite the popular antagonistic association, every professional should be familiar with sales concepts, theories, and techniques. Although you can't earn a Bachelor of Science in Closing or a Bachelor of Arts in Negotiating, almost every career path is affected by sales at some point.

Yes, that's right. For all of the engineers, creative types, and any other non-sales people in the company who think they don't need to know about sales? Guess again. There is a direct correlation between sales and revenue. Therefore, a significant decrease in sales means a decrease in revenue. And what happens when there is a sharp, consistent decrease in revenue? You guessed it: layoffs abound. Fortunately, the opposite also rings true. Make a great product decision and see sales increase and your company grow. Each and every employee has the ability to affect the company's sales.

Still, many non-salespeople are ignorant when it comes to the science of sales. *Create a decent product, find the best salespeople around, and watch those profits rise. No need to pay attention to the "how" behind selling! That's what the salespeople are paid to do! Let them figure it out. Right?* **Wrong**. Ah… for us salespeople, if only it were that easy.

Because there is often a very large disconnect between salespeople and non-salespeople, non-salespeople can make the job of sales that much harder. Personally, I've sold around, excused, explained away SO many more things than I care to admit because someone on the non-sales side of the business didn't think about what it meant to actually put the product into someone's hands and have them use it and feel value of PAYING for it.

This book primarily addresses sales in start-up companies. It speaks to both the entrepreneurs who have never had to live life on the firing line of sales, and to salespeople living in a start-up world, perhaps without the full experience of an established sales organization. That means that while you may not be a sales person, or ever had to live and die by quota, now the entire fate of your venture is going to rest on the shoulders of these evil salespeople – and you will (or should) figure out how to get into their heads. We are a strange bunch, I'll give you that, and we think and operate very differently than other people – but we are the way you are going to survive and thrive. We are also the way you will not be diluted when you go back to the investors for more money or better yet, we may be the way you NEVER need to go back to the investors. You will suddenly understand all of our pain. And... like it or not... the entire process of running this start-up will turn you INTO one of us. So, welcome to our club.

This book is about helping you get there faster – and therefore helping your company succeed faster. This book is also about helping your salespeople understand you – so make sure you make them read it too. Start-up CEO's often hire less experienced salespeople, and also expect non-salespeople to get involved in the process (if they are smart). Therefore, the faster everyone is on the same page the faster you will succeed.

Swingers? What does that have to do with anything? That will become evident as the story unfolds, but essentially selling in a start-up is about YOU as much as it is about your company. What happens when the story of you isn't all that great or clean? Your story, be it good or bad, certainly has the potential to affect the sales cycle. Keep reading and learn how to ensure your story doesn't besmirch the selling process.

PRIMER FOR THE NON-SALES CEO

The basic tenets of sales are critically important, no matter your title or experience. You need to sell and your company needs to sell. You need to attract the best salespeople. And the best way to do it right and not waste your time? Really understanding what makes salespeople tick.

If you are a salesperson or a sales manager in a start-up, you may feel inclined to skip this section. I advise you against doing just that. CEO's and sales managers need to be on the same page as salespeople. That is exactly the point of much of this section. If nothing else, this section will help you with the words to explain better to the CEO what's going on in the sales cycle and sales team if they haven't read this book.

So you have started a company or want to start a company. That's excellent. Welcome to the world of entrepreneurs. I will go into more detail later, but here is Rule #1: Having a product is VERY different from having a company. What separates a product from a company?

SALES.

Most startup employees do not list hard-core selling experience on their resumes. In my experience, former-salespeople-turned-entrepreneurs are a minority. And truly great salespeople willing to work at a start-up? They are even more rare. Why?

Most salespeople want to make a ton of money. Great salespeople do. Therefore, they typically have less drive to go and build something new. If someone is successful, earning a great living, and enjoy what they do, there would be little to no motivation for him or her to become an entrepreneur.

A person in this position is even less likely to jump ship to work for your startup. On top of not being able to match their previous base salary, your budget likely does not cover travel expenses, technology, and other tools they require to do their job well. The opportunity for commissions is also low because the product is likely unfinished or untested, as is the market. Why would they work for your startup for peanuts and a dream when they can sell a tested product and rake it in? The reality is this:

The more successful the salesperson, the less likely they are to want to come to your startup.

Clearly this is not a hard and fast rule, and there are plenty of exceptions, but the odds are that if you are starting a company, or working for a start-up, you have never been an extremely successful salesperson.

If the world of early-stage startups has a dearth of really great salespeople, how are sales going to be the lifeblood of your company? How do you attract those people I said you couldn't attract, and how do you think like them? How do you begin to understand them so you can motivate them?

That is what this section is about; helping you discover what it means to be a salesperson, even if you have never "carried a bag."

THE LANGUAGE OF SALESPEOPLE

One of the most interesting things I've found in my dealings with entrepreneurs, who have never been salespeople, is how many common sales terms are foreign to non-salespeople. As in any profession, there are specific concepts you must understand if you are going to be able to effectively communicate. It's very important for you to fully understand these terms. It's the first step in understanding what drives, motivates, and moves salespeople. It offers a glimpse into how we view the mechanics of your business. It exposes the best approach to negotiate with salespeople and get us to do what you want. It's the only way you can get us to *take* the challenge of selling your product - if we know you will think of things on our terms. Demonstrating your devotion to thinking on our terms will pique our interest and elicit a better response. This list is by no means exhaustive, but contains most of the terms that are critical to know.

OVERARCHING SALES TERMS

Quota: A quota is the amount of sales that the salesperson is expected to hit within a defined period of time. Quotas may be set by month, quarter, annual, or otherwise, but it is the target that you expect the sales person to hit. Every great salesperson will want to *crush* this number. For reasons we will further explore later, setting this number is an art, not a science, and will be the subject of much debate. Since you don't have a long track record of sales, this number may be a semi-educated guess or driven by investor-led goals.

Carrying a Bag: Having a quota. It's a cheeky reference to the traveling salesperson, but salespeople use the term to describe people that have sales quotas and have lived under the pressure of a quota. You, as a CEO and/or founder of your company may have "sold" some deals, but have you ever "carried a bag?" If you haven't lived the "make a sale or don't pay your rent" life, then you have not carried a bag. In terms of dealing with salespeople, you should honor the fraternity of people who have lived and died by making or not making sales.

Pipeline (Funnel): The list of potential sales. Every company should have a pipeline of deals. Lots and lots of potential deals need to come into one end of the pipe, move through the pipe, and come out the other end as closed deals. Sometimes this is called the "sales funnel," representing that a great number of deals go into the top of the funnel, but that number is whittled down as they move closer to a close. Marketing, business development and sales all work together to build the pipeline, but ultimately it is sales' responsibility to manage and maintain the pipeline. Sales managers will know roughly what their "close percentage" should be at every stage, and will look to make sure that the pipeline has enough deals in it to ensure success relative to the targets (quota) set by the company. As will be discussed later, pipelines are strange beasts in start-ups because there is no predictable sales process. Such a deficiency makes drawing conclusions for a pipeline very difficult. Nonetheless, it is still the key tool for any salesperson and sales organization. Whether it be in a sales force automation tool, an online spreadsheet, or a piece of paper, the pipeline is the list of deals that the organization is working on and is the key indicator of performance, second to the number of actual closed deals. Each salesperson is responsible for his/her own pipeline. Sales managers will be responsible for the pipeline of all their direct reports (and perhaps their own deals.)

Making Rain: Great salespeople are known as rainmakers. They make things happen that shouldn't be possible.

Inside Sales/Outside Sales: These terms refer to the type of sales person and function. Generally, inside salespeople work their sales solely by phone. They do not leave the office to make their sales. Outside sales people go to clients and do a great deal of their sales work outside of the office. Outside salespeople may do a large percentage of their work inside the office as well, but they will go to a client if and when they need to. Some of the best inside salespeople are not comfortable standing in front of a room of people, but they are great salespeople when they are on the phone.

Sales Cycle: The sales cycle is the entire closing process from beginning to end. When someone asks what your sales cycle is, they are referring to the average amount of time that it takes to close a deal. Some products have a very short sales cycle, and others have a very long sales cycle. This is going to be a big unknown when you start selling your product, but it is a crucial indicator of sale performance and in predicting cash flows from sales.

RFP/RFI: When selling into large corporations, Request for Proposal and Request for Information are large documents that must be filled out with extensive and detailed information on the company. Sales people will need the assistance of a great number of people in the company to complete these documents. You should not expect that your salesperson will be able to fill this out alone, but you should expect them to guide the process.

CRM (Customer Relationship Management): Every company should be using a CRM tool to capture information on all leads, prospects, customers, etc. The database serves as a way to identify, organize, and assign leads. It also tracks the progression of customers as they go through your pipeline. It is important to make sure data gets put into the CRM, as it is the only place that this data will outlive your salespeople. You want to make sure that nothing is lost if and when your sales people transition out – and that you have the simple ability to transfer those leads and customers to another salesperson. Salesforce.com is the most popular option; however, there are many other excellent choices on the market depending on your needs.

LeadGen: The process of generating leads for the sales person to act upon. Sometimes this is a very structured process, and sometimes salespeople are responsible for generating their own leads.

Individual Contributor: Sales people are often referred to as individual contributors when they are not in management. Sometimes, sales managers are expected to sell as well, and this term refers to the people who do nothing but sell.

Empty Suit: Sometimes, managers are inserted into the sales process with little to no understand about the sales process. These are referred to as empty suits. We also refer to this as the Sales Prevention Department. Avoid being an empty suit as much as possible.

Save Face: Sometimes, as salespeople, we have to go back on a promise, or have to adjust a deal based on poor performance of the company, etc. Saving face is preserving a relationship and your integrity with both interested parties.

Champion: This is the person in the company you are trying to sell to who likes and wants your product and is helping you on the inside. It is important to try to find a champion who can help you close the big deals.

Landmines: Anything that can trip up your deal. This could be something as simple as your champion changing jobs, and sometimes is something about your product or offering that ultimately kills your deal. You need to try to navigate around the landmines as much as possible. Great salespeople will plant landmines for their competitors. For example, he/she may say in a sales meeting, "As I'm sure you have seen in your investigation, the robust offerings all provide you with two-pass authentication to avoid hacking into your sensitive data. Oh... three of them don't? Interesting, I'm not sure how they can support an account like yours." Usually this sales person knows EXACTLY what he/she is doing, but is planting that landmine which he/she hopes will blow up most of the competition.

Murder Board: The training technique of flushing out holes in your pitching process by acting as the worst customer possible to the sales person.

Pain: Salespeople talk about customer problems in terms of pain. What pain do you solve for the customer? While your solution may do 100 things, if it solves 1 major pain of the customer, he may buy it. It is the salesperson's main job to identify that pain so he/she can solve it.

PIPELINE STAGES / CUSTOMER STAGES:

Understanding and agreeing on the definitions of different stages of the sales process is critical to a happier sales force, and less confusion on any particular sale.

Prospect: A prospect is anybody that you haven't sold to yet. These are people/companies that *may* want to buy your solution but are not yet customers. While both customers and prospects need to be treated with respect and care, you should always recognize the difference between the two entities.

Customer: Someone who has closed a deal with the company. This may or may not be a paying relationship. If you decide to give away some portion of your product for free, that person is still a customer. The distinction is that the person has agreed to do business with you – regardless of the financial transaction.

Opportunity: An opportunity is a deal in progress. Once a salesperson knows that there is a potential deal to be closed, it becomes an opportunity. In an initial transaction, a prospect and an opportunity are tied together, but in all future transactions with an existing customer are opportunities.

Account: An account is usually a customer or a prospect. Depending on the sales structure, and the type of product being sold, an account can be a one to one relationship with a customer, but not always. In other words, you might be selling to a single account, but have prospects in several divisions. Some divisions may become customers while others stay prospects.

Lead: A lead is any potential prospect that is identified by marketing, business development, sales, or other. Leads can come through a web site, mailing, direct contact by the lead, etc. Once the salesperson reaches out to the lead, it may be classified as a prospect or unqualified.

Qualified Lead: A lead with whom a salesperson has communicated and determined there is a potential fit for the product. At the qualifying stage, some sales teams will require the determination of the existence of a budget, the identification of a decision-maker, and other information that indicates the chance that a particular prospect has of purchasing the product in the future.

Unqualified Lead: A lead is deemed "unqualified" once it has been determined that this prospect absolutely cannot and will not use the product. The lead may be deemed unqualified for a variety of reasons, but once the lead is disqualified, it is no longer handled by the sales team.

Closed: A deal with the existence of a signature acknowledging an agreed relationship. This may be an electronic acknowledgement or otherwise, but it is a deal in which there is no doubt that the customer has agreed to establish a relationship with your company.

Lost: Any deal in which the customer has expressed that they have decided not to buy your product, or the salesperson has given up any and all hope of closing the deal (the customer disappeared.)

Verbal Commit: A verbal commit is when a customer tells you verbally that they have decided to purchase your product. Sales people will rejoice at the verbal commit, but know that even though someone tells you they will buy, many of them will not. The verbal commit is a very important sales step but it should NEVER be confused with an actual closed account.

COMPENSATION TERMS

On-Target Earnings (OTE): This is the amount of money a salesperson brings home in salary and commissions if they exactly hit their quota. This is the best metric on which to compare and judge different job offers so it is a critical measurement. One company may offer a salesperson $50,000 / year plus $50,000 in commissions if they hit quota for an OTE of $100,000. Another company may offer $75,000 / year plus $10,000 in commissions if they hit quota for an OTE of $85,000. The initial comparison will show that job A is probably better - because if quota is set fairly, even though there is less base salary, the opportunity is better and the commissions are probably higher so there is more opportunity for accelerators. The OTE gives a salesperson a reasonable expectation as to what they should earn if they achieve the quota that you have set for them. It's the best way to compare two positions.

Accelerator: The commission rate post-quota. Typically companies will provide a commission rate up to quota and then an accelerated rate post quota. For example, if every salesperson is supposed to sell $1 million in new business, and the sales person is paid 5% of every deal, they would make $50,000 in commissions on those sales. This company may pay 8% for every dollar sold post quota. So for the second $1 million sold, the sales person would make $80,000 in commissions. This may initially seem painful to watch more of your margin taken away, but if you can get salespeople selling 1.3x or 1.5x or even 2x of what you need them to sell, you will not need to hire as many salespeople and you will save money in the long run.

Draw: A draw is guaranteed commissions granted to the salesperson when they are first hired. While we will go into more details further on in the book, the basic concept is that it will take a salesperson several months to sell and receive commissions, so salespeople are often granted draw as a sign-on bonus to cover them until they have a chance to build a pipeline of sales. The concept of a draw will be further examined later in the book.

Up-side: The reward the salesperson gets for taking on the risk of a lower salary and overachieving.

Sand Bagging: The art of holding back sales during one period and moving them into another period so as to optimize the payout of the compensation plan.

Claw-Back: Commissions are very often paid up-front to salespeople and for good reason. However, sometimes, in order to make sure that salespeople are smart about the sales they make, they are expected to ensure the customers will become long-term customers. The details are below, but the "claw-back" is the ability for the company to reach back and take back some of the commissions that have been paid out for a customer that doesn't work out and can be tied to a sales-related issue.

Override: The commission made by a sales manager from sales made by his direct reports.

If you become an entrepreneur, you are already a salesperson. The first sales you make are to…

- Your spouse, significant other, and other family members who will be joining you on this risk – perhaps mortgaging your future, sacrificing vacations and other things to go on this adventure.
- Your investors. You need to sell your vision to your investors – be it friends, family, angels or institutional investors. You must prepare budgets, timelines, estimates, return on investment (ROI), business plans, market analysis, etc. This requires heavy and detailed research.
- Your employees. It is crucial that your employees fully comprehend business objectives, products, timelines, expectations, personal responsibilities, etc. Your employees need to share in your passion and faith in the company. They also deserve to know why they are jumping off this ledge with you.
- Your bank, landlord, vendors, and others. All parties involved need to understand your vision and why it is beneficial for them.

Therefore, you will be the first person developing the sales pitch. It's unlikely that you will get it right at first, but you need to be developing this pitch in your own mind, and probably in deck form as well. By going through this exercise, you are building the foundation for a sales pitch your sales team will eventually further develop. A good sales team will tweak it and own it, but it is the entrepreneur's responsibility to provide a strong foundation. The best way to test out your pitch is to give it over and over again to potential customers.

When you ask someone to come sell for or with you, it is imperative that you have absolute faith that people will definitely want your product. You have to fully understand the pain that your target audience feels and empathize with them. If you can't do this, then there is little chance for your company. Therefore, you need to make the first sale. You need to find someone, ANYONE, who wants your product and is willing to pay for it. If you can't find a single person that thinks there is value, then it is incredibly unlikely that you will have a successful company.

It's entirely possible that you haven't quite figured out how to get the deal over the finish line, and entirely possible that you can't grow from more than that single customer, but you need to be a major part of that first sale. Entrepreneurial sales are about selling your vision, and you must to be able to communicate that vision, get other people to not only buy it, but also share in your enthusiasm. If you can't get a single customer, then there is little to no chance that a salesperson can make it happen either. Great salespeople can make rain, but they can't often make people want a product that has no market.

Every salesperson that follows the founder will need to be able to draw on the success of those earlier sales to show that there is indeed a market need for the product

MANAGING SALES IN A STARTUP

One of the most arduous tasks for an entrepreneur is managing the sales effort – and I mean the entire effort – not just the individuals in sales, but the entire sales process. The sales process, especially in a start-up, affects the company in its entirety.

You must weave the sales team into the sales process and the company vision, and make sure that they are moving the company where you want them to move it.

In this section, I'll discuss topics including how to get your team onboard, the best ways to coax the team to drive company goals, and how to keep them motivated.

One of the first major tasks that you will need to do is to recruit your sales team. This is one of the most difficult and frustrating parts of running a start-up – as well as one of the most expensive. Not because salespeople are expensive, as we will explore in the compensation section, but because BAD salespeople are VERY expensive.

What should you look for when hiring a sales candidate?

Most people will tell you that when you hire a salesperson, you should look for confidence, persuasiveness, intelligence, an extensive Rolodex, and the persistence of a two-year-old. Sure, all of those things are great (less the Rolodex), but you are talking to **salespeople**. We are not normal. By nature, we are trained at our core to manipulate conversations, control the direction of conversations, and make you feel good about what we saying. Not to mention our superhuman ability to seduce you into believing that you are not really looking for the attributes you thought you were. No, instead, you are seeking exactly what we have to offer. Our job is to close you – to get the deal done.

So how do you find the right people? It is very, very tough. I am an experienced sales manager and I still get hires wrong about 30% of the time, too. There are some clues that I use to find the right people that I will list below. In the next section we will discuss how to make sure that you are constantly evaluating and making sure that those people you hired are the right ones.

ROLODEX REQUIREMENTS ARE HOGWASH

I find it amusing that the word "rolodex" is still in the lexicon. I don't know of any professional salesperson who still uses one of these devices. Yet, they still sell these things! Who is buying them? Are there salespeople who store their most valuable information source on handwritten cards on their desk? The salespeople you want are fluent in Microsoft Outlook, Apple's Address Book, salesforce.com, SAP, Microsoft Dynamics, Highrise, SugarCRM, or any of the other fantastic digital CRM products that exist to manage contacts.

Rolodex has never released, to my knowledge, a successful digital product. Yet this is still the word we use to refer to your contacts, your connections, and your network.

This brings me to my real question; if you are hiring a salesperson, what is the value of their "Rolodex?" How much emphasis should you place on who they know in **particular** companies? One of the single largest mistakes a company, start-up or not, can make is to request a potential salesperson to "have an established network of contacts in XYZ industry" or "bring a book of relationships" or anything of the sort.

In most cases, the idea that a salesperson's contact list contains some sort of treasure trove proves to be false. Given the fluid nature of business these days, I can guarantee you the contact information in their "Rolodex" is mostly outdated. I'm not challenging the idea of finding someone with a broad network. But I strongly caution against relying on someone's Rolodex to immediately affect sales in particular companies.

When people stayed at their jobs for 50 years, having connections inside a particular company had value. Today, people move around so much, it's unlikely that the exec I know at company A will be there long - or his power may quickly shift. Add to that, Hoovers, data.com, and other tools have made the organization transparent. And tools like LinkedIn have broken down the walls of knowing who the decision makers are - and have WAY better and more current information than what is trapped inside a person's "Rolodex." The value of knowing people in a company and building a lasting trust within that company is certainly less valuable than it was during a time when people stayed at their company. Budgets and initiatives are squeezed and you may know the CEO of company A, but that will less often lead to a sale than it may have in the past.

I am certainly not suggesting that there is NO value to a person's network. But here is where the shift is now. It is less important to me that you have contacts at companies A, B, and C that may possibly get me a sale. What I want to see is a person who understands the value of networking and has done a good job of it. What is the reach of your network? How have you used it - and how will you continue to use it.

When evaluating a salesperson, I want someone who knows the sales process. How do they get the sale completed? This, to me, is of far greater importance than the people they know at a *particular* company. In my career, I've sold into several industries: aerospace, high tech, insurance, trucking, fashion, venture capital, entertainment, utilities, banking, direct marketing, and more. In almost EVERY situation, I've had to start without a pre-filled set of contacts to call - yet I was successful in beating into every industry. Why? Because the focus was always on the sales process: finding the right solution for the customer and communicating it; Understanding the way to determine and traverse an org chart (using the digital tools mentioned above).

And… using my "rolodex" of people to get into those organizations when needed. Yes, my contacts were almost always part of the equation – but never the answer.

If selling is building a big fire, then your Rolodex is simply the kindling. It's up to you to stoke the fire and make it burn. And when no kindling is available? *You still have to make the fire.* THOSE are the people I want on my team - the ones that can make a fire WITHOUT kindling. In this economy, with executives moving so quickly, you will probably find more situations without kindling than you do with kindling.

So, as you evaluate the salesperson you are about to hire, ask the right questions. Check his/her network; ask about sales he/she have made and how he/she did it. Which networking groups and **meetups** does he/she attend? How will his/her network help you get sales faster?

Don't think that finding someone with a plastic contraption with names and numbers on it is going to solve your sales challenges.

I'd take a great salesperson who can network over someone who knows 15 people in an industry ANY DAY on my team. Learning how to sell and how to find new people to sell to is 150 times harder than calling 15 people you already know and asking them to buy your new product. The fact is, even if you know 15 people, the odds are, at best, that only one or two will buy it. Then you are back to needing someone who can reach out to new people. So, again… who do you want on your team?

Take this idea a little further and you will find that great salespeople can learn new ideas and industries very quickly. So, which is better? Someone on your team who can pick up sales pitches easily, creatively create new pitches, and can find the value of customer needs or someone who is so entrenched in a single industry that they don't have any reference to how the rest of the world works? Having worked in so many different industries, I clearly think that someone with broad experience is MUCH better. But it's the **core sales ability** that is the most critical.

As I debated the Rolodex idea with someone, I explained what I thought the Rolodex of the 21st century was – your sales network and your sales reach. When I look for a team member, there are many traits (like expensive hobbies) that I look for, but I've really begun to understand the value of the team member's sales network.

Recently, a connection of mine sought me out for some sales advice. They had a particular question about how to sell to an account to which I had sold contracts valued at millions of dollars. I was able to quickly tell this salesperson exactly which process to use to close the deal:

- How to navigate the organization.
- How the purchasing process worked.
- How to circumvent the "approved vendor" requirements.
- How to arm his champion with the information he would need to sell it up the chain.
- And more…

This person was selling a COMPLETELY different product from a COMPLETELY different industry, but my advice still helped him close the deal.

Rolodex? OK – yes he had me in his "Rolodex," but not in the traditional sense of what a Rolodex means; I was not a sales contact to whom he could immediately sell. I was a person in his Rolodex who could help him make the sale to a prospect outside his Rolodex.

This is the function of the modern-day Rolodex: to genuinely connect you to the people in the sales realm who can and will help you get the information needed to make the sale. It's about who can give you the advice for that industry, that product, and that pitch to make those sales easier and faster.

So, my first and most important advice to a hiring sales manager is STOP LOOKING FOR A CANDIDATE'S ROLODEX and start looking for their reach and their core sales ability.

It is significantly easier to learn your product, your industry, your pitch, and navigate to decision makers than it is to learn how to sell.

It doesn't matter how specialized you *think* your industry is – great salespeople will be able to sell anything because they stick to a sales process of value, they know how to open doors and how to get people to believe. A great salesperson will learn your product and your industry very quickly and be productive in sales just as quickly. A mediocre salesperson who knows your industry will remain a mediocre salesperson. Look for talent in sales, and forget industry and Rolodex. Those things mean NOTHING towards your success. I've sold in mobile, logistics, ecommerce, collections, finance, venture capital, legal, gaming, advertising, and more… and rarely did I start with a Rolodex. But in most instances, within 3 months, I was hitting and/or my team was crushing quota. This fact is true for ANY great salesperson. The Rolodex does not matter.

Look for talent in *sales*… forget their Rolodex.

EXPENSIVE HOBBIES

One of my most read blog posts on QuotaCrush was about an off-hand comment I had made at a lecture on sales strategy. Someone asked me the number one qualifier that I look for, and honestly, without thinking, I responded that expensive hobbies were the absolute most important thing that I look for in salespeople. I don't think I thought about it fully before I said it, Even though it was a knee-jerk response, as I spoke, I realized that it truly is a great qualifier I have used quite often.

So what does it mean to look for expensive hobbies?

Determine if the sales candidate participates in expensive **LEGAL** hobbies. Obviously, I do not mean an expensive cocaine or heroin habit. I mean skiing, scuba, spa, golf, biking, expensive watch collections, expensive purse collections, etc. These are things you can usually glean in the banter that occurs before the interview starts.

Expensive hobbies speak to two things:

- They have had some previous success that allowed them to partake in these hobbies.
- They have motivation to repeat that success in order to maintain those hobbies.

You need to sense a *massive* passion for that hobby. I don't mean just skiing, but someone who has decided they need to ski every mountain around Lake Tahoe more than once, and at least once on every continent that has skiing. I don't mean someone that enjoys biking, I mean someone that describes the bike they own (or REALLY want to own) as having automatic transmission, disc brakes and made of titanium. It is that type of passion for a hobby that typically tells me that this is someone who is driven, focused, and squarely thinking about cash in their pocket at nearly every turn. The more this salesperson craves that hobby, the more she/he is going to be thinking about closing. This is, of course, good for you.

The single-handedly best salesperson I ever had working for me? She had a serious addiction to designer shoes and handbags. During our Monday morning pipeline calls, she would tell me about some pair of shoes and some handbag she saw that weekend, and how she needed to close two deals this week to afford them – but rest assured she was going to do it. Was she motivated to close the deals because I needed her to? Slightly. Was she motivated because she needed a job? Partially. But her main motivation came from Chanel, Dior, Jimmy Choo, Manolo Blahnik, Hermes, etc. I really didn't care what the drive was within her – but the drive she felt for that possession was more motivating than anything that I could provide her externally. She had a personal drive that was symbiotic with my need and the company's need.

When you meet a salesperson, ask about what they do outside of work. Even casually bring it up as you sit down for the interview... "It was beautiful this weekend, did you do anything fun?" Have the picture of your daughter's tennis championship visible on your desk to invoke a conversation about sports. If they bring up golf, ask where is the best place they ever played or if they have ever gotten the chance to play in Scotland. Strike up the conversation and find out where their passion lies.

If they have no passion for life, or the enjoyment of it, then I would be so bold as to say I do not think that they would be a great salesperson.

CREATING THE PITCH ON THE FLY

One of the most interesting proof points in evaluating salespeople is one that illustrates a key difference in the mind of a salesperson versus other business people. On several occasions when I was doing sales consulting, my clients and I both interviewed a candidate and came out with vastly different opinions.

The cause of this disparity usually related to the questions the candidate asked, primarily relating to the product and how it is pitched. The more questions the candidate asks about how we are selling the product, to whom we are selling it, and how the product works, the better I feel about the candidate. In contrast, non-salespeople often see this as a sign that the candidate did no research, understands nothing about the industry, and is so clueless that they could never be successful. However, this is not necessarily the case.

I expect that a salesperson won't quite understand our approach, product, or industry. As previously mentioned, this is not the most important thing to me. What I want to see is how this person thinks. As a start-up, our sales materials are likely weak, unvarnished, unclear and in need of tweaking. Perhaps our entire industry is nascent and there may be few parallels for the salesperson to use as a comparison. Under these circumstances, it is entirely understandable, if not expected, that a candidate would not have a firm grasp on how to sell our product based on the available information.

During an interview, if a candidate asks a lot of questions about how you pitch, how you sell, and the like, she is mentally developing her individual pitch. She may not fully comprehend your product or the product direction, but as the conversation progresses, a good salesperson should propose suggestions on how to pitch the product, or "have you tried this approach" questions. These suggestions are often WAY off your corporate mission but that's OK. From a sales perspective, this manner of interaction implies that the candidate **knows how to listen**, is able to digest the information, and devise a creative solution. The salesperson that is building his/her pitch the minute he starts hearing about the product is **already thinking about how he/she can close deals**. This is the key to the entire thought process. A salesperson who is thinking about a solution that leads to a close is the salesperson you want on your sales force.

When this salesperson gets into sales meetings for your company, they should be able to bob and weave around the questions thrown at them. If they are someone who is willing to creatively think about your product – even in a way that wasn't originally intended, they can often find the way to sell it.

There is a danger in taking this too far, which will be discussed in the "Sell What We Got" section, but the key, especially in a start-up, is to find the salesperson who is not afraid to build a pitch in the interview. You may have to reel them in, but creative thinking and listening ability are critical

I EXPECT YOU TO VISIT MY WEBSITE

The flipside to this argument is that I do indeed expect you to have at least done surface research about the company and the industry. The information age has created a monumental amount of information that salespeople are expected to use. As I will discuss in the Sales Tactics Section, research must, must, must be done on every company and every person you are going to speak with prior to a sales call. There is no excuse not to do this research, and because the information is available, companies expect you have used it. (Full Disclosure: I founded a company called FunnelFire that provides this research to sales people in a proactive way.)

Therefore, if your candidate hasn't done any research on you, you can be sure that they will not be one to do research on their prospects.

I called a candidate once who had an impressive resume and he said to me, "I'm sorry, I've applied to so many jobs in the past week, can you remind me what you do?" Now, if I had called him out of the blue, I would have perhaps given him a pass, but this was a scheduled call and he didn't take the time to even research what the company did before I called him. My reply? "My company FunnelFire is about helping people be prepared and clearly you are not. This interview is over."

As I mentioned in the "Creating a Pitch on the Fly" section, I wouldn't bash someone for not understanding everything correctly. That will be something you can work on as time goes by, but they should have some semblance of what you do – and who you are as the interviewer. I write a blog called QuotaCrush. If you do a web search on my name, my blog is one of the very first links you see. If you go to LinkedIn and look-up my name, QuotaCrush comes up right away. If the salesperson I'm interviewing hasn't seen that or even read my latest post? I highly doubt they will take the time to do the research required of a salesperson.

HIRE TWO AND FIRE ONE

One of the largest expenses that a start-up will encounter is on failed salespeople. That is why I always recommend hiring two at once. It is easier to train two people at once and the pair will develop a sense of camaraderie. Ultimately, you will reduce your start-up effort for salespeople. If you are looking for one sales person, hire your top two candidates. If you are already hiring multiple people, try to add one or two more for insurance. Failure to catch on is a real problem so this provides you some insurance against that failed person.

If after 3 months, you find that one of the people you hired is not working out? You can fire them without having to start from scratch. Chances are, the other salesperson is working out. Of course, it is entirely possible that both people fail, but less likely.

If you are lucky and BOTH salespeople are succeeding, well then... bonus! But regardless, the protection is worth it. The cost of not having a salesperson for a short amount of time typically exceeds the cost of hiring two at once.

When hiring however, make sure you never more than double your team at one clip. If you have one salesperson, aim to hire one more (using rule above). If you have two, never hire more than two at a time. If you have four, never hire more than four at a time. Before you plan to hire again, make sure that your team has stabilized. Adding salespeople when the rest of your team is unstable and underperforming is a sure fire way to kill your sales mojo. Hire, get your team working well, and then hire again. If it isn't working, determine who needs to go, and then trim and replace. Don't feel the need to expand if it isn't working yet. It won't lead to more sales.

GOOD VS GREAT

Throughout this book you will see that I refer to good salespeople and great salespeople. There is an endless amount of good sales people. You do not want a *good* sales person on your team.

What is the key difference between a good sales person and a great sales person?

The ability to close deals that bring in cash...

consistently

It's fairly easy for a person who is somewhat familiar with the sales process to get people interested, generate sales orders and have a lot of excitement about your company. The hard part is actually getting money to leave the customer's hands and enter yours. This is the small action that separates good sales people from great.

Think of the typical sales environment that everyone loves to hate – the car dealership. It's easy to get you looking at a car; it's easy to get you excited about a car. A great salesperson gets you to drive away with the car they sold you. A good salesperson will have you looking at lots of cars and then promising to come back someday.

So how do you know that you are looking at a candidate who is a great salesperson? Ask about actual closes.

I ask candidates to tell me about the sale of which they are the proudest. Then I ask about the hardest. Then I'll ask them to tell me about the one they lost that still frustrates them the most. Then I'll ask about one that stalled and how they revived it again.

Listen to the answers. If you hear mostly "we" in the answers, then you can be sure that this is not the person that made the closes happen. It may have been their boss, or they are full of malarkey. If the answers are "I"-based, you can safely infer that they actually did the work.

If they do not have answers to any of the questions – or no good story – then you probably do not have a great salesperson. There isn't a great salesperson on the planet that hasn't lost a deal, struggled with another, and has at least one big win they are dying to tell you about. "There really isn't one deal that I can remember stalling and I've never lost a big deal" is a lie – no matter who says it.

The rest of the content relating to which process they utilized can be interesting and telling, but not critically important. It should make sense and it shouldn't all be accident – it should be a process that the person thought through and eventually led to the win or loss.

Good sales people get stuck when the deal gets hard to close. They don't know how to break the logjam. Pay attention to whether they know how to finish deals and get the money into your bank account.

GREY HAIR OR BLUE JEANS

I would never advocate age-discrimination, and my grey hair reference is more about experience than age, but you have a serious choice in which person you hire for your sales roles, and you also have to decide which roles you really need. Do you hire someone who is experienced in sales or do you hire a junior, super-energetic salesperson.

Of course…you want both! Often you can find an experienced salesperson with energy to spare. But what we are really talking about here is COST. An "experienced salesperson," is a euphemism for an EXPENSIVE sales person. A proven, grey haired, salesperson who has closed numerous large accounts, has earned the right to a higher base salary – especially at a start-up where there is so much risk. Such an experienced salesperson can easily go to a more established company and make a lot of money.

This means start-ups have the tendency to find less expensive salespeople whom they believe (hope) can pull it off. And many will be able to do just that.

Take me, for example. I started my career as an entrepreneur, selling my software. I had no experience in sales. I was a programmer. Yet, I figured it out and was able to close some very large accounts. I also lost a lot of accounts along the way. I was fortunate to have some experienced sales people by my side that gave me tons of great advice along the way.

If you follow this route and go with a more junior salesperson, you will be paying for on-the-job experience, so how do you best mitigate this dilemma to get the sales you need.

The options, as I see them, for a start-up are:

•   If you have a CEO or other management type who has hard-core sales experience, then hire the junior sales person and save yourself some money. And I mean real quota carrying sales experience – not just an ability to sell. That manager can guide and train the salesperson, help them avoid the obstacles, power through objections, and quickly get up to speed on how to close deals. Without this, you are likely to get lots of activity – but not lots of money. A new salesperson typically needs their energies channeled – especially near the end of a sale because that is when it gets hard. The path of least resistance will take their activities to new prospects where all conversations are lovey-dovey. Managing activities and the pipeline are going to take a portion of the CEO or other management person's time, but having management oversight will be critical – or lots of cycles will be burned without sales.

- If you don't have a management team member that has done hard-core sales, then hire yourself a true VP of Sales. If he/she is all you can afford, then that VP of Sales can carry a quota until he/she makes enough sales to justify another team member. While this person will cost you more money than a junior salesperson, you will actually be spending money wisely. This person should more than make up for their expense. He/she should be able to set in place the right sales structure, and get some anchor accounts that will cement your sales strategy moving forward.

- Hire the young salesperson, and then have an external advisor that is a sales guru (board member, outsourced sales management firm, partner firm) work with the salesperson and manage their activities. Get the experienced person involved early on. He/she can shape the strategy and guide the junior sales person. This junior salesperson, if conditioned to rely on the advice of the expert, can be guided by the senior salesperson in terms of what steps to take next, when to call again, how to handle certain objections, which accounts to prioritize, how to get past a gatekeeper, how to break a log-jam, when to negotiate on price, when to know you are getting the brush-off, etc. He/she can also be the grey hair to call in when they call in their senior management for either a webinar or a face-to-face. If you have someone committed to the success of your company, this can be a great option for a start-up. If you have angel funding, you may learn that some of your angel investors can be, and would be willing to be, this person to you. For many years at QuotaCrush, this is exactly what I did. I helped multiple start-ups accelerate their sales by relying on me to provide grey hair guidance to the blue jeans sales staff.

It's certainly a tough decision for a start-up, and the costs surrounding sales (not just salary but travel, entertainment, etc.) are difficult pills to swallow. But like in anything else, it's not wise to go cheap on the sales side, unless you can back-up the junior sales people with some real sales management. I honestly believe that companies with great sales typically have solid sales management and structure behind it.

If you opt to have, or are finally ready to have a sales manager, you need to clearly define the activities that the sales VP will be carrying out. It is my VERY strong opinion that having your sales leader responsible DIRECTLY for quota is a bad, bad idea.

Imagine a football team: the coach is watching his offensive line, looking at each play carefully. He sees his strategy working. It is second down, three yards to goal! But he pulls his star quarterback and subs in... HIMSELF! The crowd is deafeningly silent. There's the snap... he has the ball in his hand... and he scrambles for the touchdown! The glory is his - forget about that quarterback and offensive line he spent his precious time training! This touchdown is his - boosting his stats and running up his tally of points! The coach looks around, expecting his team to praise him, possibly hoist him onto their shoulders... but all he sees are annoyed stares and the tension is palpable.

Later in the game, the team is in another predicament. The clock is running out, the opposing team has had a strong run and is within field goal length of the win. The team looks to the coach for advice on which play to run. But... where is the coach? He is off on the side warming up in case he has to run another play and hasn't been paying attention and has no advice for which play to run at this critical juncture. When the team presses him for a decision, he makes a quick uninformed decision so that he can get back to his own tasks.

Now back to sales. Instead of a coach, you have your sales leader. Instead of a quarterback, you have your salesperson, trained by your sales leader and working hard to close sales. And instead of a touchdown, it is the large account your salesperson has worked tediously to close. The dynamic between your sales leader and new salesperson mirrors the one between the coach and his quarterback. Is that dynamic productive, positive, and successful? Probably not.

When you ask your VP of Sales to carry a quota, you are essentially doing the same thing. That VP of sales will, or it will be PERCEIVED as he/she will, cherry pick the best, most profitable, and easy to close deals that come into the organization. It doesn't matter that the reason the VP may be closing these deals quickly because that VP has tremendous sales experience; the team will view it in another light. If you ask the VP to carry a quota, you create a negative dynamic amongst the team.

Second, the sales manager who carries a quota has the same crunch-time pressures shared by all of the sales representatives. This means that at crunch time, unless already way over quota, that manager will be working like mad to close his own deals. Will that manager be able to be the sales tool needed to help his team close deals? No. If the sales manager has the opportunity to earn an accelerator, will he care about the override on a smaller deal of another salesperson? Unlikely.

I once worked on a team where the VP of Sales had his own quota, and whenever I needed him, ESPECIALLY when I needed him to help me close a deal, he was not available. He had his own challenges – and he made more money when he closed his own deals than when he helped me close mine, so his focus was elsewhere. The entire team essentially worked around him and knew that we could not count on him.

The better way to do this is to have the VP of Sales assign every deal to his team, and then have the VP partner with salespeople on each deal. Let the salespeople run the deals, and the VP can be as involved as he needs to be – even running a majority of the deal, but leaving the administrative and follow-up to the sales manager. This gives some corporate leaders heartburn because they think they should not have to pay two people commissions, but as I will dive into, it's always better to overpay when you are just getting going.

SALES VS BUSINESS DEVELOPMENT

As you decide what types of sales people you need in your start-up, it's worth mentioning the difference between business development and sales.

In the traditional sense, business development people deal with creating channels, partnerships, and strategic opportunities for the company. Sales are the people who go and get people to give you money for your product.

Since "sales" can have, in some people's minds, a negative connotation, there has been a trend to call salespeople "business development people." In my opinion, this is a sorry effort to create the illusion that the function of salespeople is not to convince people to give them money. True business development people often have no revenue quota, and instead are managed by objectives. So, by tagging someone a "business development" person, you, in theory, are making their contact with potential customers less threatening.

However, I think that the core of every successful sales strategy is one of honesty. If you are starting the relationship as dishonest, then you are starting on the wrong foot. **If you are tasked with going out and finding revenue for a company, you are a salesperson.** You can call yourself an "account executive" or "account manager," if you are tasked with establishing and maintaining relationships, but you should always be honest about the fact that you are trying to get them to purchase your product. In my entire sales career, when people asked me what I did, I said, "I run sales for XXX" or "I'm in charge of sales for the north east region," etc.

I've never been a ruthless salesperson. I'm always looking for the win-win of selling value, but I never hid the fact that the entire reason I was having a conversation with the prospect was to determine if there was a way that I could improve their business – and that they were going to PAY me to do this.

I am not slamming business development. Business development is an important function in every company – especially start-ups. And, very often a company will have business development and sales under a single person or department. In those cases, I believe sales AND business development should be in the title to eliminate any confusion.

The bottom line is that I object when the term "business development" is somehow used to trick the customer into thinking that the sales person is not a sales person, but trying to find some "partnership" with the firm. If you are looking for a way to get someone to pay you for your product, you are a SALESPERSON. And it's OK to be proud of being a salesperson. Salespeople bring tremendous value to clients and companies.

The question you need to ask yourself is "What types of interactions am I going to have with my clients?" If you are asking your clients for cash, then you need salespeople. If you are looking for partnerships and doors to open as a path to clients, then you need a business development person. Perhaps, and most likely, you need both. Be clear on whom you need for your company and how you are expecting them to deliver it?

Remember that the differentiator between a good salesperson and a great salesperson is the ability to get cash in the door. Usually, it's that difficult last step of asking for money that trips up otherwise good salespeople. Good salespeople are very often great business development people for that reason. The close is often an easier ask and less difficult to get agreement on. So, as you evaluate what it is that you need in your company, make sure you think about that when you evaluate your candidates.

DETERMINING THE RIGHT MIX

Now that you hopefully know which types of people and personalities you need on your team, you also need to find the right mix of people and positions. The mix can include inside and outside salespeople, business development people, leaders and individual contributors.

What you need for your product is not something that can be defined generically, and it may change as your company changes and grows. The key is to make sure that you know what each type of person can do for you, so that you can properly experiment and find your perfect mix.

MOTIVATION & COMPENSATION

Getting the salespeople on board is only the first step. The hard part begins when you try to get these salespeople to make actual sales. Some of the challenge is because, well, you are a start-up. You are figuring it out along with the salespeople, and part of the challenge is that unless you are a seasoned sales person and sales manager, its really difficult to know how to motivate sales people, how to know when they are manipulating you, when they are failing, and even when they are succeeding. In a start-up, your sales process will and should be very fluid as you figure it all out. This unfortunately will cloud some of what is making the process work or not work – so your job will be that much harder.

Salespeople are primarily motivated by compensation. Setting the ideal compensation that both ensures you get what you need for your salespeople and correctly builds your company can be tricky business. But it is imperative that you do it properly if you want to retain and attract the best salespeople as you grow.

SALESPEOPLE ARE FREE... AREN'T THEY?

When done correctly, salespeople should be a no-brainer addition to your workforce. In theory, if you add a salesperson, they reach quota, and if their compensation plan is designed correctly, the net result to the company is more money in than out. You should, in theory, be able to add as many salespeople as you can and it will only mean more money in the company bank account, right?

If you run an established business, in an established market, with established pricing, a mature lead generation program, etc., then this is mostly true. The problem is that most of the above is not true for your start-up. Your compensation plan isn't going to be right, your product will pivot, your salespeople will be inconsistent – and there won't be enough successful ones in the beginning to absorb the failures of the bad ones

But, the objective should be to get the sales effort to at least a break-even point as quickly as possible. Once you break even, aim for profitable. Once you do this, you will have the ability to hire more and more salespeople while knowing it means more revenue in the bank.

Be prepared for a short-term loss while you figure it out, and understand that your investment will be worth it in the long run.

YOUR STOCK IS CRAP

As we start to build out the components of compensation, we should get the stock options discussion out of the way. Entrepreneurs frequently include stock options as elements of compensation packages. They believe they are building an amazing company and therefore assume that all employees, especially salespeople, should want to work all hours of the day to make the company a success. As a token for all of the hard work and late nights at the office, they offer employees a piece of the company.

It amazes me how many entrepreneurs want to hire a great salesperson yet don't do any math before making an offer to that salesperson. If I'm taking a job with your start-up, it's likely for less money than at an established company. And my odds of making commissions are much lower because well... we aren't quite sure whether or not anyone wants to buy it, or who wants to buy it, or what the right price is, etc.

All of this is fine, right? Because I've got stock in your company? Well, let's assume everything goes well and I'm at the company long enough to vest my stock and you sell for a nice number. The amount that I get from that company sale had better way exceed the cash I'm giving up to work for you. If I can make $250,000 more in an established company with an established product and sales channel each year, then your stock had better make up for that in spades – or at least have the appearance that it will. I should feel as if I can make two or three times that number to make up for the risk. Yet, entrepreneurs will attempt to offer stock to salespeople that wouldn't even come close to making up for the ability to make lots of commissions elsewhere in the meantime even if the company were to sell for a large number. This is the math you must do if you want to attract the best.

It is not that salespeople don't want stock, and it's not that we don't know the eventual value of the stock if we help get it there. But, sales people know that it is a "what have you done for me lately" profession, and that you are liable to get fired for a few bad months. Yet, in a start-up, it may be because the product was built wrong, or we asked you to sell to the wrong market, and by the time we figure that out – you are fired. Therefore, no salesperson really counts on the fact that they will ever vest or otherwise see any real benefit to the stock options you are offering. We can't count on it the way other people can, because we are MUCH more likely to be gone before we vest even if we have done amazing for a long time, short term blips can still get you fired. Your stock is a magical bonus to the salesperson if it ever becomes something, like a lottery ticket is put away, but is certainly NOT considered much when evaluating the offer.

Sales motivations are about cash now – while you can get it. Tomorrow a competitor may be better than us, or collapse on pricing, etc. Any of these could lead to our demise. Again, it's about the cash. How much of it can we get today?

If you see articles and studies arguing that people want to be challenged and have freedom more than they want cash, don't believe them. I will guarantee you 100% that no salespeople were consulted in that survey.

COMPENSATION

Now that we have established that salespeople are all about how to get cash, you understand why the concepts behind proper compensation matter so much.

It may seem crazy, but every great salesperson will spend a portion of every day thinking about how much they have made, and what they can do to make more money.

You need to create a compensation plan that is aggressive and challenging, yet achievable and fair. If you do this, you will see amazing production from your team.

There are several components to compensation as it relates to salespeople. While I've covered a lot of the terms in the beginning section, they are worth reiterating before we delve into each one, exploring how each impacts sales motivation, relates to the psychological dynamic of a salesperson, and affects your sales team.

- Base Salary
- Commission
- Accelerators
- Draw
- SPIF (Sales Performance Incentive Fund)
- Spot Awards
- Quota Club

BASE SALARY

Base salary is the most obvious of all the component terms, but perhaps the most misused component when it comes to salespeople–especially in a start-up.

Base salary is our guarantee, our ability to know that there is at least some chance that we are going to have money to pay rent and eat this month. Salespeople are expected to perform by making sales. When they succeed, they receive significant reward in the form of commissions (see next term). Because of this potential, often there is a desire to not pay a base salary or make it unreasonably low.

This is a very bad practice for a start-up. Working in sales is hard enough when it's for an established company with an established track record and known pricing, target market, etc. When you are trailblazing, it's even harder. And when your salespeople are concerned that they are not going to have enough money to pay rent, they're not spending as much brain-time on selling, researching prospects, etc. It's important to provide some sort of a base in order to ensure productivity.

And you should NEVER do commission-only deals in a start-up. While it's very tempting, it won't grab the attention of the right, successful, great salespeople. Salespeople who accept commission-only jobs are usually naïve, desperate, or frauds. Commission-only salespeople seldom make a significant amount of sales because most of them will not be focused on your business unless it is already a repeatable sale – which is rarely the case in a start-up. Once in a blue moon, you may find a salesperson who has been so successful that they don't care about a base salary and can be successful. However, most of those people also believe that if you aren't willing to put any money into the sales effort, that it's a bad omen for any ongoing success of the company.

If you want performance from a salesperson, you are best served by offering a small but reasonable base that allows the salesperson to reasonably live. You will get reduced performance if the base is too small, culminating in a potential for near-zero performance if you pay nothing on the base side.

COMMISSIONS

Variable compensation is the lifeblood of any salesperson. This is why we got into this profession, and the more we want it, the better we probably are at it. We see variable compensation as the ability to turn hard work and longer hours into more cash in our pockets, which is something that many people cannot experience in their professions.

In the very plain sense, a commission is the percentage of a sale that you pay to the salesperson. Many people will ask me what commission rate they should pay, and this is a very difficult question to answer generically because the effort of the sale, the price of the product, and so many other factors weigh into this question. As a rule of thumb, if a salesperson is performing exactly the way that you want them to, they should be able to double the amount they make in base salary. Of course, if you have elected to pay a very conservative base salary, the reps should be able to make more than double in commission. If you provide a generous base salary, the commission can be a lower percentage.

Commissions should never be capped. I will repeat this. **Commissions should never, EVER be capped.** It is absolutely mind-boggling to me that any company, start-up or not, would decide that a salesperson has sold enough and is no longer eligible for commissions after a certain point. When you cap commissions, you have defined a point where **a salesperson will stop working**. There will be no incentive for them to continue, until the cap is released. If you want more sales within that time period, you will need to rely on other salespeople to deliver it or release the cap. You will have to pay more base salary, more benefits, and take on more risk with a salesperson that may not work out in order to bring in the same revenue. There is no logical reason in the universe to do this. The best idea is to allow and encourage your stars shine as brightly as they can.

ACCELERATORS

Once a salesperson hits their quota of sales, they are typically rewarded with an accelerated commission rate. For example, if they are receiving 10% of every sale up to quota, they might receive 12% of sales after they have reached quota. This is an incentive that salespeople receive to continue selling after they get to what we "need" them to achieve. People who receive accelerators often help make up revenue that underperforming salespeople don't get for us, and they also allow us to reach our growth goals without hiring more people. Both situations are good for the company, so we want to reward these people accordingly.

High performing salespeople expect accelerators and will focus on them because they know that this is their "cha-ching" opportunity.

DRAW

Draw is compensation offered to a new salesperson coming on board. The "draw period" is the time over which the draw is paid (typically 3 to 6 months). There are two types of draw:

- **Recoverable draw**: This is a set amount of commission that is paid to the salesperson in advance of actually being earned. It is pre-paid commissions that get credited against earned commissions. If, at the end of the draw period, the salesperson has not sold enough to cover the amount of the draw, then he/she needs to pay the company back the unearned portion of the draw.

- **Non-Recoverable draw:** This is a set amount of commission that is paid to the salesperson in advance of it actually being earned. At the end of the draw period, the salesperson is NOT responsible for paying back the un-earned portion. Think of non-recoverable draw as essentially a higher base salary during the draw period that drops down after the draw period is over; however any actual sales commissions made during the draw period get credited against the draw.

Sometimes draw is a series of set payments. Draw may also be available as an option, allowing a salesperson to request it if and when they want it. This option is most popular when the draw is recoverable. Under these circumstances, a salesperson may hold off on receiving the draw if they feel they may be at risk of having to pay it back.

Why do salespeople deserve draw? Isn't it all about their performance? A salesperson should just work harder to receive their commissions more quickly, right?

Some of that is true, but the fact is that sales compensation plans are designed to drive behavior. They should always be designed to drive the behavior that the company wants. As a component of a compensation plan, draw can be a very important part.

The most important thing that you want your salespeople focused on is SELLING. Use draw to eliminate distractions and stressors and facilitate a smooth on-boarding of the salesperson. If a salesperson is worried about getting their first sale in time to pay their mortgage, they won't perform or focus as well. Once the salesperson has built a pipeline and is moving - then it's all up to their performance.

There are many situations where draw makes a lot of sense. Some examples:

- *Your product has a long sales cycle.* If a realistic time frame to close a deal is 9 months, even if you have a superstar salesperson, you know that it will be several months before any sales are made. It is reasonable to offer a draw to help that salesperson stay focused on selling in the initial 6-9 months.

- *The salesperson is walking away from large commissions.* One of the hardest things for a salesperson switching jobs to do is walk away from the large pipeline he/she has worked hard to build, as well as the large potential commission payout. If you really want this person selling your product, you can offer a draw to compensate for that loss of income. This is essentially a signing bonus – but tied to sales in your firm. In fact, I'd rarely recommend a signing bonus but would often recommend a draw to this type of salesperson.

- *Your product/market/pricing is not established.* Of particular relevance to start-ups is asking a salesperson to come on board and trust that your product has a market, that the pricing is correct, that your product works, etc. For all these reasons, it is reasonable to offer a draw to a salesperson while he/she flushes all of that out. You don't want the salesperson to be thinking about moving on, stalling your momentum, because he is too focused on when he will start making commissions.

- *Your comp plan is mostly commission.* If you are offering a compensation plan which is very low base salary and mostly commissions, a draw can make sense in order to make sure the salesperson has some income during their startup phase.

While you should be expecting big things from your salespeople, remember that EVERY salesperson has a start-up phase and it can take a while before he/she sees a commission check – not because he/she is a bad salesperson, but because pipeline building can take time. When a salesperson is walking into a virgin territory, new product, etc., it is reasonable to offer him/her a draw to make sure that they stay motivated and focused while they get up to speed. In fact, offering a draw can help ACCELERATE sales in the short term because you keep the salesperson focused on selling.

Since draw, both recoverable and non-recoverable, is credited against actual sales commissions, if the salesperson does succeed in the short term, then you don't double pay the salesperson.

Should you offer recoverable or non-recoverable draw? This is really part of your negotiation. Of course, non-recoverable is better for the salesperson and recoverable is better for the company. Asking for the recoverable money back at the end of the draw period certainly is a de-motivating exercise; however, it protects the company in the event the salesperson really cannot perform. In my own experience, offering up non-recoverable vs. recoverable is based on the person and also the maturity of the product. If I'm confident in the sale-ability of my product (already proven it can be sold), then a recoverable draw makes sense. If I'm working with a known entity (the sales person has succeeded in 10 other companies), then a non-recoverable draw may be more appropriate – because if he/she doesn't sell it's a function of my product and not him/her. Relatively green salespeople should probably be offered recoverable draw until they prove themselves.

Bottom line: There really are no hard rules around this. Draw should be part of negotiation with the sales rep. Start-ups need to be realistic about the task they are asking the salesperson to undertake. And while they are getting risk/reward for their sales efforts, it is essential that steps be taken to keep them focused during the start-up phase for an unproven product with a virgin market and untested pricing. A draw may make the difference between you winning or losing.

SPIF / SPOT AWARDS

Within any month, a sales manager should have tools that they can use as part of their plan to move different items. Sales Performance Incentive Funds (SPIF*) and spot awards are some of the most important and effective tools used to motivate salespeople.

---

* "SPIF" can be used as a noun or a verb, depending on the context.

In a large company, the CFO would typically set aside an amount of money, a SPIF, with which a VP of Sales could use at his/her discretion to move the needle on particular sales items. A VP of Sales could create challenges and then use that money to incentivize different things. Unlike established sales firms, start-up firms are not likely to set aside specific funds for this purpose, but it is always a possibility. Even if you don't set aside those funds, you might still make use of essentially the same idea in the form of a spot award.

The best way to describe the use of a spot award is in the following examples:

- **Sparking a sagging team:** Perhaps the entire team is having a down month, and you are trying to spark the team. *"I'll give a $100 cash to the next salesperson that brings me a signed order"*
- **Shift sales focus***: The next salesperson that brings you a signed order in a particular industry that hasn't seen a sale in a few months gets to take Friday off.*
- **Drive over-achievement***: Two plane tickets to Bermuda for the top salesperson who is over quota this quarter, provided that two or more salespeople are also over quota.* This will drive those who have already achieved quota to keep going more and more and can lead to top performers trying to best each other.
- **Drive team behavior***: If the team when considered all together doubles quota, and 80% of the team hits quota, then each person on the team gets $500 cash.* This type of incentive drives team behavior and can also lead to stronger salespeople helping weaker ones since 80% of the team needs quota.
- **Encourage proper tool usage***: Each salesperson that maintains the CRM perfectly this month gets a free copy of Sales, Swingers & Startups and an iTunes card.*

I could list lots and lots of examples here, but essentially the take-away is that you should have in your back-pocket ad-hoc awards and compensation, which are very often NOT cash (and sometimes of no cost to the company), to help redirect effort in a particular area and help drive overachievement.

The last major component of any compensation plan is the Quota Club. This is something rare in start-ups and typically reserved for more established sales teams, but it is something that start-ups should consider as part of their overall sales management and compensation plan.

In a large sales organization, the Quota Club (or President's Club, or other elite name) refers to the set of salespeople who in the previous year reached their quota. This should be the set of your best salespeople – those whom you would like to see stay on your team because they have delivered at least what you expected of them and likely more. In large corporate settings, this often refers to a trip that is taken perhaps to Hawaii or the Bahamas (spouses & significant others included). It is a large celebration and a good way to let off steam for those salespeople that worked hard, forsaking their personal life to make that quota.

Clearly, in a start-up, you are not going to be forking over cash to a large trip like this one, but I do think that you should be considering some sort of Quota Club for those performers that you want to retain. Perhaps quota club members are afforded half-day Fridays in the summer provided they are still above quota. Or perhaps quota club members reach their accelerator at 90% of quota this year instead of 100%. Yet another idea is to offer up perks like first grab at certain leads or an invite to the company off-site strategy session, or other insider incentives.

Quota Club should be used as an incentive to retain the best salespeople by giving them an extra incentive to stay above and beyond the cash that they are likely making.

BRINGING IT TOGETHER INTO A COMP PLAN

Now that we have briefly gone over the components of a compensation plan, the key is to tie it all together into a comprehensive compensation plan that achieves the goals of the corporation and is also fair to the sales people.

The most important thing to know in a start-up is that you will, with almost near certainty, get your compensation plan wrong in the first couple of tries. Why? Just as your product will likely pivot from the user feedback, your compensation plan will need to pivot based on those product changes, feedback you get from your clients about how they want to pay, and what you learn about your sales cycle.

Considering all of the elements that we have discussed, the key is bringing them all to the table to get a plan that gets the performance you need.

How exactly do you do this?

I wish there was a magic wand on this, but there really isn't. The best way to build a successful compensation package is to put something out there, see where it goes, and be willing to change as you see how it works.

But you need a starting point. To get started, you need a couple of pieces of information:

- Your corporate sales revenue target, if you have a defined one
- An idea of how many sales you realistically expect each sales rep to make
- The price(s) you expect to sell at
- A rough idea of how long each sale will take

When you first start out, you will have none of this information, so you will need to research based on your competition and comparable products. There are also a lot of standards out there for different types of companies. For example, Bessemer Venture Partners, a prominent venture capital firm, has some very comprehensive reports on how to best compensate cloud services. In general, they advocate paying the first month of a 12-month contract in a recurring revenue business.

A good general rule of thumb, a starting point is paying about 8% on sales. You should lever that up and down depending on your price point, and you should make sure that sales reps have a reasonable chance of doubling their base salary.

PLANNING FOR FAILURE

When you design your compensation package, a common mistake that sales managers make is to plan for perfection. In other words, if the company needs to bring in $500,000 in revenue and there are two sales people, the inexperienced manager would set quota at $250,000 per sales rep expecting that each rep would bring in half of the desired revenue.

In actuality, this is very poor planning because you may lose a sales person, a salesperson could get sick, external forces like competition or a market crash, or lots of things could happen with can disrupt the sales cycle. You should never plan for perfection. What you should do is give yourself some buffer so that you are shielded from those inconsistencies or failed salespeople.

In general, you should take your sales goal and inflate it by 20% and then divide that out. Continuing our example, if you need to bring in $500,000 in sales, then ask the sales team to bring in $600,000 ($500,000 x 120%). Each sales person would be assigned $300,000 as quota. If both salespeople reach quota, it's a great year. If one fails or something else happens, you are hopefully much closer to your goal then you would be otherwise.

PAYING THE SALES MANAGER

Over the years, I have had a lot of companies ask me about the best way to calculate what to pay a sales manager. It is actually quite simple. Considering a sales manager should never be both a coach and a player, the sales manager should simply be getting an **override** on the sales team plus a base salary. (and of course, you can also pepper his/her comp plan with spots and SPIFs too)

This means that when the sales rep makes a sale, the manager gets a commission too. Not the same percentage, but a small piece above it.

For example, if the sales reps make 8% commission on each sale, then you might give the sales manager 1% on the sale. The sales manager will earn this on each and every sales rep that they manage. This gives her the incentive to help ALL of their reps close ALL of their deals. It will force her to take deals that she could be working alone and assign that work out to his reps so she can help close many more deals than she could otherwise.

Accelerators for the manager should be corporate and team driven. For example, you may offer an accelerated override rate of 1.5% once the team quota is reached and/or 80% of the sales team reaches quota.

PAY ON PROFIT OR REVENUE?

An interesting question that continuously comes up is the basis for commission. Should you pay based on the amount of profit that the sales produces? Or should you pay based on the amount of revenue that the project produces?

In general, I always advocate the goals of the compensation plan must match the goals of the company. When these two objectives are in alignment, the sales team can be very productive, and everyone wins. When these items are mismatched, frustrations on both parts are likely to emerge.

The question you need to ask yourself in order to answer this main question is: What is your objective for sales this year? Is it revenue or is it profit? While this seems like a silly question, it really isn't. Companies, particularly start-ups, often have a need to generate market share and anchor clients. Companies may be willing to take certain clients at any cost for the sake of counting them as clients – and often certain products are loss leaders needed to get companies started before they get the more expensive products.

Once you know what you as a company want to achieve, then you can set your goal appropriately. When you set it incorrectly, your sales team gets frustrated and de-motivated. For example, in one of my sales jobs, I was in the process of landing a large consumer packaged goods company as a client. This company, for most companies, is such an amazing anchor account that most would do whatever they could to get a deal with them. Ultimately, this is what my management was telling me to do. In fact, they had me present a proposal that included a gaggle of free services. I was able to land the account, but got nearly no commission on the deal because my compensation was based on profit – not on revenue – and once you factored in the free services that we had to offer, the profit was squeezed out of the deal. I managed a sell few follow-up deals that did generate me some commissions – one a rather large deal – so I was okay in the end. Even so, I was a disgruntled salesperson for quite a while because I was doing an awful lot of work for no commission. Had the company really thought about what they were asking me to do, they could have re-worked the compensation so that I was whole on this deal because they wanted it so badly.

When you are primarily concerned with market share, you should probably pay on the revenue that is generated rather than profit. If the salesperson is focused primarily on profit, this will be contrary to the goals of the company, which are to gain a client base and some market share. The company position might be that they would be willing to take a client at any price above a loss (and perhaps even some special situations at a loss), yet a salesperson would see that deal as an unworthy effort.

Ask yourself this question, "What will you think if a salesperson walks away from a deal because there isn't enough profit for them to make any commissions?" If the answer causes any angst over the salesperson's decision, then you should be paying on revenue. It's obvious that you want sales that produce even a small amount of profit. If, instead, your answer is that you would be happy with the salesperson's decision, then commission on profit alone. That will ensure that the salesperson only goes after deals that generate a significant amount of profit.

MORE MATH = LESS SALES

A salesperson who used to work for me called to get my opinion on a new position he was considering. We chatted for a while about the position and the opportunity. I was very excited for him. It was (and is) a great company, a great product, a great team – and it was an amazing opportunity to advance his career.

Then we started to figure out if the comp was right for him.

He explained to me the compensation plan that was presented to him. As he spoke, I said, "wait… I have to get a pen and write this down so I understand." OK – the fact that I had to say this is 100% a clear indication that this is a bad compensation plan – but nonetheless I attempted to understand the plan. The plan paid out upon a rolling average of monthly sales over a three-month period and provided incentives on this and that.

After I thought about the plan for a while, I said, "OK. I get it and from my calculations, it's most likely a very generous plan – but it's sort of hard to tell – and it's going to be very hard to know what you will get until the end of each quarter."

I certainly appreciate that the CEO of this company was trying to create a generous compensation plan, and I honestly think he believed that he was encouraging the right behavior. Nonetheless, the problem with the comp plan is twofold.

1) It is too difficult to calculate and know what one is getting paid on each deal. The sales rep will spend too much time thinking about what he will or will not get paid instead of just focusing on closing.
2) By making the plan based on a rolling average, the "cha-ching" factor after a deal is closed is gone. When a deal is closed, what does it mean to the rep? No one knows until the end of the quarter, so it's not as exciting when a deal closes.

Here is one of my most basic rules on comp plans. Make them simple and easy to calculate. Give me a cha-ching when I close that is very clear on what I get and when I get it. This will motivate me to close more sales more quickly. I see something I want? How do I do it? Close a deal at this amount and I will get enough to buy it. Want to make more money than that other salesperson. How? Close deals totaling X to get there. This is how we think.

The more time I have to spend on math, the less time I spend on closing. The more time I'm wondering about what I get paid, the less likely I am to close it. When I don't know what it's worth to me personally – I have less drive to bring it home.

Perhaps these sound like strange concepts to non-sales types, but this is what motivates us. The hunt. Make it like a hunt and we will hunt it down. Make it like a complex problem with too many goals and triggers and we will be less motivated and driven.

In one of my sales roles, the CEO decided that he wanted us to bring in sales more rapidly throughout the year, so while we had an annual goal, he wanted to reward MORE the people who brought that money in sooner rather than later. So, the basic intent was that two sales reps could bring in $1,000,000 each but the one who closed the deals faster would make significantly more money. The plan went roughly something like this:

- Take your annual quota and divide it by 12 to get a monthly quota.
- When you make a sale, look at where you should be relative to the cumulative monthly quota, and then create a ratio of your cumulative sales and the quota.
- Take that ratio and apply it as a positive or negative factor to the commission rate and that is the rate at with that deal will get paid.

My brain actually hurt trying to remember that convoluted sales plan. This CEO was so proud of the plan and really thought he was going to excite us to sell more. The sales team's entire reaction when we closed deals was, "You know, I really have no idea what I'm getting paid on this. The client wants a price drop. Ah screw it, just give it to them. I'm probably not making any commission on this deal anyway." I kid you not, it was probably the worst incentive plan I have ever been underneath, even though the intentions were good.

The flip-side of this is one instance where I created a compensation plan that paid a straight commission and one that increased (slightly) with each subsequent sale. The sales reps that worked for me could easily calculate what each would get paid on each and every deal. There was no question, and the fact that each subsequent deal got a tiny bump made each subsequent deal that much more exciting. To add to the excitement, the entire team knew what everyone else was working on and therefore felt the challenge of wanting to rise to the top.

Create exciting plans that challenge salespeople and make them compete and cooperate. Get them excited about hunting down and closing deals. Don't make them do too much math in figuring out what they get paid.

HOLD US TO FACTORS WE CAN CONTROL

When you look at things to compensate on, make sure that you do not factor in things that are out of the salesperson's control. When you do this, you cause angst and anger within the sales effort.

In the crazy math compensation plan described above, there was yet another wrinkle in the compensation plan that I did not mention above. The "close" date at which you could calculate your compensation was the day at which the company could bill for the services that were sold, NOT the day that you signed the deal.

At this company, the tech team was very backlogged - for a good reason. The sales effort from the previous year was very successful, and most large ticket items had a bunch of highly profitable professional services customizations (which the company had compensated on in the previous year in a desire to build up that team and its revenues). The problem was that this team was incredibly backed-up, and new projects got added to a massive backlog while they hired new people and got projects out the door.

In one instance, I closed a deal on January 8th. Signature on the piece of paper, negotiated, funds allocated, etc. Considering the compensation plan, this was a massive win for me. It was the equivalent of one third of my annual quota which, given the incentives to bring in cash earlier, would have been massive for my commission plan. But, the teams were backed up. My project was delivered in *October*! I actually got a negative commission ding on this deal and many of my other deals that year because they got *delivered* late even though they were *sold* early. As you can imagine, I was incredibly mad at the professional services team, and from January to October was a constant nag to them. And unfairly on their side, EVERY sales rep on similar issues was slamming them. Why? These people were directly affecting our compensation and we had absolutely no control over what was happening, if it was happening, and if it ever actually got done. Since I worked over 1,000 miles away from the home office, I was certainly not staring them in the face to get my project completed and mine was often punted for other projects of salespeople they DID have to face each day.

In post-mortem analysis of the situation, I can see that this compensation plan directly led to the animosity between sales and tech, and it wasn't necessary. Design your compensation plan on things the salesperson can directly affect. This will be different at each company, but honestly ask yourself, are your reps are in charge of a particular aspect or are they at someone else's mercy? If they are at someone else's mercy, then avoid making that part of the plan.

I would have dealt with receiving less commission on this deal, but only on factors of which I was in control. Imagine when the client came to me asking why the project was late, and the tech team begging me to give them more time... was my incentive to help push the delivery out? Absolutely not.

COMPENSATE EVERYONE FOR SALES SUCCESS.

In the early days of a very successful software company, they had a rule that each and every person within the company would get a piece of the commission on sales made by the sales team. The result was an entire company firing on all cylinders to get sales completed.

In the vignette above, about the overworked professional services team, I can tell you that they had a chip on their shoulders because the sales reps were making all this money on these sales, and they had to do all this work to make it happen. But, I can also tell you they rarely worked weekends or late nights, except when they were forced to. This is not a slam on these people; this is the way that their pay works. You get the same amount of money if you work 40 or 80 hours a week. You get the same amount of money if you do three projects in a month or if you do 12 projects in a month. Do your best, but there is certainly less incentive to crush it.

If this company had taken the above example, they would have given these people reasons to over-achieve. If it works for sales people, can't it work for everyone?

Give the programmers $100 each time a sales person closes a deal and they do the work necessary to get the customer live. Give the marketing department a cash bonus for each lead that results in a sale. That certainly gives them incentive to make sure that leads are of a high quality rather than just "a lead." Give office support staff a bonus when they rush through the contracts, or get the credit card processing problems worked out. The list goes on and on.

You are in a start-up and you need to have the entire company in sales mode. In a small way, put everyone on a compensation plan that is symbiotic with the sales compensation plan and get the entire team working together.

BRIDGING THE START-UP GAP

Another thing that you should clearly be looking at as you devise your compensation plan is bridging the gap that comes with the start-up phase. Much of what is discussed is the plan when you are moving along well and sales are happening. But, when you first start out, you won't have a full pipeline of companies to go after, you will take some time researching them, getting your lead generation moving, and then you may start to get some initial meetings. You'll miss wildly on some efforts, and win on some others.

You should be very aware of the challenges that your sales team will have in the beginning and be looking for ways to short circuit them and help out the team in any way that you can. It's not uncommon for start-ups to forgo a particular quota, or offer accelerated commissions in the beginning months or in difficult times. Using the tools we have described to make sure that the engine gets moving is critical.

It is very easy to simply push pressure down on the team, and expect magic, and in that sense you will likely churn thru quite a few salespeople. Your better bet is to understand that you are pushing a truck up-hill and the more hands you have to push that truck, the faster it will get there. Once it's at the top of the hill and on flat ground, then you can expect that the sales team will do anything and everything to accelerate it.

EXPERIMENT & CHANGE, JUST NOT TOO OFTEN

All of these ideas on how to design compensation plans all boil down to one basic tenet of sales: the compensation plan drives the behavior that you want from the sales reps. If you want market share, then design a plan that emphasizes activity. If you want Fortune 500 named clients, then design a plan with a bonus for those clients. If you want profitable deals, then design a plan that rewards profitable deals. Just keep your plan as simple as you can and still meet your objectives.

In a start-up it is okay to experiment with different compensation plans as you figure out what works, but you need to understand that a shift in focus is very stressful on sales reps that have built their pipeline around a particular compensation plan.

Sales reps are lightning bolts. When you give us a compensation plan, we will find the quickest path to making cash, and we will go in that direction. So, when you change the objectives, it is very distracting to us and perhaps brings us back to square one. For example, if you planned to go after Fortune 500 companies, and then determine that you don't want them anymore, it's likely that my pipeline is trashed when you change that objective. If your pricing, or basic offering is slightly changed, then it may not affect your salespeople that much. You need to think about this when you change objectives.

Since you know you have to change often in a start-up and that you are going to pivot, you should set the expectations that the compensation plan is for a set of time – typically one quarter at a time – and resist making major changes within that time UNLESS you determine that no one is selling and this change is to benefit the sales effort. If a compensation plan is paying out significantly, and it is your desire to change because you realize it is actually paying TOO much and your goals and commission rates were wrong, the best bet is to let your sales team know that the plan is changing and that they should close what they can while they can.

Whenever making any significant changes that will affect the pipeline or negatively affect compensation, you should provide at least a month's notice in order to avoid angering your sales team and getting negative performance (or massive churn).

IS IT WORKING?

In the early days of any company, it can be difficult to know whether your compensation plan is working. Of course, the best indicator is likely that you are meeting or exceeding your goals. But, you can always ask yourself if I met my goals, perhaps I didn't set them high enough? Or perhaps I made the plan too easy?

I was once on a team where the Sales VP set sales goals that only 5% of us hit. At the annual sales meeting, the few of us that met the goals were treated like celebrities. I'll be honest; it felt great to be one of the few at the top, one of the few in the Quota Club, and one of the top earners that year. I knew it was going to lead me to the best leads for the next year, and be great for my career.

Once I became a sales manager, I reflected on this moment and realized how horrific this fact was: only 5% of the sales team hit goal. And we celebrated it! When I had a conversation with one of the people who was a mid-level manager at the time, he told me that it was that way *by design*. The team goals were set incredibly high so that the team would strive very hard and even if several of the team did not hit goal, then the company overall would be OK.

I said that you should not be planning for perfection, and that you should give yourself a 20% buffer. It is OK if you stretch that a little, but this sales manager gave himself a very, very high margin, and in the end, he sacrificed the long term for the short term. I know that in the next year, the churn on that sales team was unbelievably high – including myself – because it became clear, even to me, that the next year my goal was going to be impossible to reach. This sales VP was just a hired hand so perhaps he didn't care, but in a start-up, it's YOUR business and churn of great sales people (or even good sales people who are about to become great) costs you significantly more than keeping them around.

When you set your compensation plan correctly, about 80% of your team should be able to hit their quota. If more than 80% of your team reaches quota, then your goals are not high enough. If less than 80% can reach it, then you either have the wrong team or your quota is too high. It's possible, as I mentioned, that the reason the quota cannot be reached has to do with the start-up phase. But if your team is not reaching quota, no matter what, then you need to take a very close look at the quota you have set relative to the stage of your company.

When 80% of the team hits quota, assuming you have given yourself the 20% buffer, then you should come close to the corporate goals. And, because within the 80% that reach quota, you should have several that go beyond it (because you have given them an accelerator), you should be able to reach and exceed the corporate goals.

Clearly, these are rough figures and you will need to play with them, but the most important thing to remember when determining if your compensation plan and motivation are working, is if most of your team (but not all) can reach the goals that you have set. If so, you will have a happy team, and it will increase productivity as time goes on.

PAY QUICKLY AND CLAW BACK IF YOU MUST

Another common question is *when* to pay commissions. In general, you should pay commissions as quickly as you can.

In all instances, you should wait for the company to be paid, and then you should pay the rep immediately. Even if the company receives multiple payments, it will still be better for the company if you pay the rep up front.

For example, if you charge for your product over 12 months, you should try to pay the rep up front in the first month – even if the rep gets most or all of the revenue in the first month. You want to give the sales rep a quick shot of adrenaline and then have that rush be gone.

The worst thing that you can do is to create any type of recurring revenue stream for the sales rep. In any month that a sales rep makes NO sales, they should receive NO commission payments. They need to feel the rush and the shame of their sales performance in a close context to when it happened. I once worked with a client who insisted that the sales rep needed to receive a percentage of each payment as it came in rather than give it all up front. Near the end of the year, the company was struggling, and many sales reps were underperforming. Yet, each and every one of them got a commission check. I honestly believe that when the sales started to get hard, the reps felt a little less pain because they knew some extra cash was still coming in.

There are instances in which you will expect the sales rep to assist in retention. The recurring model is again a great example. I had a client who looked at his business and realized that as long as a client was a client for five months or more, that client was a client for a long time. When a client left before five months, surveys led us to understand that they somehow thought the product was different than it really was – that the sales reps had perhaps not done their best job at explaining what people were buying. This led us to conclude that if a client stayed on for five months, that the sales reps had done their job.

As a result, we decided that the compensation plan would reward reps for keeping clients on for four months. After five months, we decided that any churn was not a result of the sales effort, but actually a result of the product not fulfilling the client needs for the long term. The way we paid the reps was to give 100% of the commission in the first month after payment, but give them credit for 50% of it. They would then receive 12.5% credit each month for four months. If a client left before 5 months, we would **claw-back** the percentage of the commission that was not earned. Rather than requiring the sales rep to actually pay the company back, the credit was taken off of future commission payments. This resulted in the nice "cha-ching" feature of a good compensation plan, paid the rep as quickly as possible, but kept the rep focused on the retention. Had we paid him out over 5 months, we would have created an annuity where he could have received commission payments in months where he had poor performance and as we discussed, this is less than optimal.

It is true that if the sales rep leaves the firm, you lose a chance to claw-back a certain percentage of the sales if someone drops off, but this is a small price to pay for the instant gratification feature of the compensation plan.

SMILE WHEN YOU PAY

When you design the right compensation plan, you can have top salespeople making a lot of money and the more they make, the BETTER it is for the firm. My first company was a very sales-driven company. To that end, I was overjoyed when I had to pay a large commission check. Why? Because that means a BIG sale was made! Big sales meant big money into the company – which benefited everyone related to the company – employees, investors, and customers.

When I served as VP of Sales at one company, I was (and still am) pretty proud of how the compensation packages drove performance. When I compared Q1-Q3 for the year before I worked there and compared it to Q1-Q3 of the first year I was there, the improved compensation plan nearly TRIPLED the sales performance over that time. The same team did three times what they did a year before and the offering was the same, the price was the same, and the prospects were the same. The only thing different was the compensation plan and the VP. Sure, it cost the company more money in commissions, but you can't argue with that kind of performance increase.

What makes this story even better is that I went back and calculated, given this year's performance and last year's compensation plan, what the old plan would have paid out. The new plan that I put in place actually paid out slightly less than if the old plan was in place – but because of the design and the use of the levers like spot award, SPIF's and accelerators, the plan drove increased performance.

The lesson here is that it is not only about what and how much you pay, it is about how you use the compensation plan to excite and drive behavior in the team.

Designing a proper compensation package is quite challenging, but when you do, rejoice as you pay out big commission checks because it means the company is doing well!

It can be very difficult in running a start-up when you are paying yourself nearly nothing to see sales people receiving large commission checks. It is natural to want to figure out how to stop/slow it down. You need to look at the bigger picture when this happens. A salesperson making a lot of money and is bringing in a lot of revenue, which means your company will survive, your stock value is rising, and your likelihood of an exit is more real.

Make sure your plan is delivering the results you need, but be happy when you see salespeople making a lot of money.

LOW SALES IS FAR WORSE THAN HIGH COMMISSIONS

I can't name a single business that has failed as a result of over-paying sales commissions. It's probable there are a few, and I'd love to hear that story if you know of one. It's certainly possible to create a sales compensation package that is overly generous – but in general, commissions are designed to be a *percentage* of sales. Therefore, by definition, if commissions are rising, then so are sales.

I want to clarify that I am talking about normally designed commission plans. I do completely understand that you can design a compensation plan that doesn't take into account the cost of doing business, etc., so much so that even as sales rise, you wind up killing your business. However, I'm not discussing here poorly designed commission plans; I'm discussing what you as a sales manager and entrepreneur are focused on when you think about paying commissions.

What will kill a business significantly faster than paying commissions? **LOW SALES**.

One time, an entrepreneur whose business had next to zero sales hired me. He looked to me for advice. My advice was to make his sales compensation plan more generous. He nearly had a stroke. He picked and prodded at every suggestion until he essentially killed all improvements I attempted to make. The crux of his argument was that he was able to identify a potential way for salespeople to abuse any improvement I was trying to put in place.

For example, there was one instance where he wanted to make sure we did not pay a sales rep double commission, even if they sold double the items to a single client. He wanted to make sure we were discounting (or actually NOT PAYING on) multiple sales. I explained that in his early stage, the last thing we wanted was a disincentive against getting lots and lots of sales. We were too young to be thinking with that much granularity. I figured out that IF every sale by EVERY rep committed this sin, he was going to pay $7,000 in extra commissions that month – and if in the unlikely instance that that was case, we could institute new rules at that point. He disagreed, because to him, paying extra commissions was the worst thing that could happen. Salespeople should NOT be allowed to take advantage of him.

I sat there, looked at him and said, "If I said that I could deliver to you the perfect sales solution for your company right now, would you pay me $40,000 on the spot?" He said "Of course!" I said, "So then why would you not risk, at max, less than 25% of that amount to let the sales reps run and maybe learn something about your product, how it's sold, how people want to pay, how much they want to pay?" He had no answer. His focus was on making sure that sales people were not paid, or unable to take advantage of a compensation plan. (His company was dead less than four months later)

Critical to any start-up is the ability to let the reps run and learn from how they sell. Another start-up I worked with experimented like crazy and paid lots of commissions. In retrospect, some of the commissions paid were probably too high – but the end-result? They are a profitable company with a great sales team and a great compensation plan. Had that client worried too much in the beginning about optimizing his process to NOT pay sales commissions, the company would likely be dead by now. Instead, he made an investment in his sales EFFORT that, yes, paid out more than it should have in some instances, but that investment has paid back in spades.

The main point here is that, in the beginning, you need sales. Without sales, you are a product not a company. Without sales, you will die. I don't think any start-up should overpay salespeople just for the sake of it – but I encourage startups to NOT optimize for NOT paying salespeople. Optimize for getting the most sales – you can always scale back if you see something is too generous.

If you do optimize and determine how to make sure that salespeople do not get overpaid, the most likely solution is that you will have a sales team that doesn't deliver breakout sales, and ultimately, a company that can't survive.

DON'T DECLARE SALES VICTORY TOO EARLY

Sales are hard.

Anyone who has done sales in a start-up can attest to that fact. Great salespeople make it look easy – or at least hide the struggle well from non-salespeople. Once a great salesperson builds their pipeline, gets down their pitch and starts rolling with it, they can easily bring companies on the pipeline, and move them through the pipeline. And they often do it with, what looks like, ease and finesse – and often with amazing predictability.

For people and managers who have never been the person on the firing line, especially in a start-up, this predictability and finesse looks like a hands down victory. And in many ways it *is* a victory. The ability to get your startup to this point means you have a product that people want and pay for. You have identified a good sales team, and they have developed the pitch, the product offerings and pricing that allow sales to happen. It seems as if sales will just happen now – regardless of who or what is in the sales role. I've seen too many non-sales startup founders think that the product must be speaking for itself, and that the sales will happen regardless of who or what is in front of them. But in a start-up, it is often the case that these great salespeople are masking the actual difficulty that goes into this sales machine. In many instances, the sales team is still pushing the truck uphill, even though the truck appears to be coasting just fine. These sales people deal with rejection all the time and focus on the positive. The message to the outside team is that everything is going well – even if it isn't. And if numbers are getting hit – or near to being hit – then it appears that it is time for a victory lap.

This is most often very, very far from the truth. The predictability that you see is often completely dependent on the people making it happen, and when you take these people out of the equation, the bottom can fall out. If you are a start-up manager, you need to resist the urge to change something that is working – even if it is costing you money – **ESPECIALLY** if it's costing you money. Since the process looks smooth and easy, the natural reaction will be, "OK, this is easy now, so I shouldn't have to pay as much in commissions."

WRONG…. **WRONG**… WRONG!!

Pay away and smile. Why? Because you've found a team that is bringing in revenue – and revenue is good. The more you are paying in commissions, the more this process is working.

True… it is possible that there are things you are paying more commission on than you should – but until you know for **SURE** that this is the case, you risk losing more revenue than you will pay out in extra commissions. I can name significantly more companies that overpaid salespeople and **succeeded** than ones that were cheap and succeeded. If you succeed and paid a little more to your salespeople, no one will care. If you fail and overpaid your salespeople, it's highly unlikely that the commissions were the reason (after all, paying commissions implies some degree of success).

One start-up I worked with tried at every turn to figure out when sales were "working" so they could scale back on what and how things were paid out. Sales were happening... but they were never automatic, and they were never easy. I was always amazed at how they would look to save a few thousand dollars in commissions, while if the salesperson left.... it would have cost them potentially HUNDREDS of thousands of dollars.

Cheaping out on a working sales team – even if parts of it feel bad – is never a good strategy in startup mode (it's actually never a good strategy for ANY company).

Given this, when CAN you scale back and change your compensation plan? If you built the plan so poorly in the beginning that you are actually losing money – I would change the compensation package right away. If the compensation package was not working to bring about the goals that you need to set for revenue – then I would certainly change the package. Once you have a large sales team that consistently makes goals – even the weakest and newest of salespeople, and it is VERY obvious that there is no large effort, then perhaps it would be time to scale it back (although again I might argue if you make your revenue and profit goals – keep it).

Unless any of that is true and if you are making money, then don't change it! This is the sign that your plan is **working** - NOT that you are overpaying, and not that sales have suddenly gotten easy.

Too many start-up sales managers are quick to declare victory..."mission accomplished," and to try to scale back what and how they pay on things in an effort to save precious cash. But I strongly warn that this is very often penny-wise/pound-foolish because a disgruntled or unmotivated sales team will not take you where you want them to take you. And, very often the reason you are paying a lot is because they are doing exactly what you motivated them to do.

Don't punish them now that they are doing it.

DECEMBER SALES PROBLEM

December is a hard sales month for companies for several reasons. The month is really only two and a half weeks long before your prospects shut down. Budgets are often used up. Vacations make it hard to close deals. Prospects are more focused on their holiday party than they are on your solution, etc. The list is long and very intuitive as to why it's hard to get sales done.

The end of any quarter is deal-making time, but December is the best of them all. I was talking to a salesperson the other day whose opinion was, "nothing happens in December." Ah, how UNTRUE! In fact, when other people slow down, it's the chance to make a big deal. But, there is a problem with December that puts sales people against sales managers. Even when both are aware of it, it still creates problems for all sides.

The problem is this: most compensation plans re-set at the beginning of the year. January is a fresh start. Close a deal in December, and the impact of that sale typically gets wiped out in only a few weeks. If you are already above quota, you get the sale at your accelerator, but if you push the deal until January, you have a running start towards next year's accelerator. If you are behind quota, you aren't going to get it at the best commission rate anyway, so might as well wait until next year so you won't miss quota two years in a row – and you will show good progress for next year.

All things considered, for a sales person, December is a not a good month to close anything. Holding the sale until January is a much better option. Unfortunately, with sales managers and companies trying to get the best financial picture for the year, this proves to be an interesting dilemma.

The initial reaction of some companies is to put negative incentives in place for the salespeople, to encourage December sales. Sales that are on the 1 yard line sometimes will get negative treatment in January to punish salespeople that don't get that sale in December that the company felt they should have (which may or may not be due to the above problem).

62

I find, in building compensation plans, motivation always works better than punishment. Regardless of what has happened in the past, if you want a salesperson to sell, put the carrot in front of them. The better solution for companies that want significant numbers in December is to recognize the challenge of the sales person and provide extra positive incentive. Some ideas:

- Bring all salespeople to the top commission rate regardless of level.
- Sales challenge for December. Put a big carrot out there for achieving a particular goal in December. Cash is best since you are combating the thought of cash for next year but a trip or other prize can work as well.
- Increased commission rate. This is a simple but effective one. Bump all commission rates up in December in order to negate the sandbagging.
- Quota Relief for the following year. Perhaps you drop a person's next year quota by $0.05 for every dollar they sell in December. This makes it easier for them to hit their accelerators in the next year.
- Immediate payment. Typically salespeople have to wait to get commissions. I've heard of some companies offering to pay immediately on December sales as an incentive because in January, they will wait on the payment scale. (This can create issues for customers that don't eventually pay – which is why I've never done it – but I figured it was worth a mention because it was mentioned to me)

I always think that you can get amazing things from salespeople if you put the right incentive in front of them.

Now, the other side of the coin is this: If you are a salesperson who is behind, and you are looking for a chance to shine – and perhaps earn some silver bullets for the next year... get out there and close that December deal – there are often dollars to grab. It will show a real effort, and earn major points for putting the company above your own personal gain.

The challenge of avoiding sandbagging salespeople in December is a very tough one. As business leaders and entrepreneurs, we want the best numbers we can get in December and for the year. As salespeople, we want to bring in sales in a way that can maximize our personal income. Marrying these two ideas is always the compensation challenge, and in December, this is a bigger problem.

SALES LESSONS FROM A 6 YEAR OLD

The best way to finish up the section on compensation is an everyday sales lesson that I got from my son when he was 6 years old.

My son was playing flag football that year. All spring and summer he frequently told me that he was really looking forward to playing flag football again. Yet, once it came time to play, he was less than interested. He whined and complained for the first two weeks of practice, and not surprisingly, gave a less-than-stellar performance on the field during the first game. After the first game, I tried to remind him how great he did last year. I made sure he got the proper rest, and the right breakfast before his second game. Again, he was a goofball on the field, and in many ways really demonstrated an embarrassing display of antics. The fact that many of the moms were telling me how cute and funny he was did not matter. It was getting me very angry that he wasn't trying his best and doing what I knew he could do well.

My reaction was to get angry with him and to punish him for his display on the field. The next week? He provided a similar display of antics. I was infuriated. But, by this point, I realized that there was a lesson here. (Indeed – it's coming back to a sales lesson). I realized that I wasn't providing the correct motivation to get the behavior that I wanted.

After his third game, I sat him down and explained to him about what would make me proud. I explained to him that I always expected him to try his best at everything he did, and that I expected the same of myself. If I wasn't trying my best at work, then my company would not survive, and that would have repercussions for all of us in the family. In the same way, he needed to always try his best. I told him that I didn't care if he got a flag or a touchdown, but that I wanted to see him do his best. Then after the pep talk, I modified his "comp plan" and told him that he would receive $1 for each flag that he got, and $5 for every touchdown that he made.

The next football game cost me $20.

I'm not sure which part motivated him more, the pep talk or the comp plan, but it worked. (Ok, he is my son. I know it was all about the cash.)

So what's the sales lesson here? Proper motivation and the deploying the right compensation plan is the best way to get the results that you want from your sales team.

Just like my son, salespeople are wired to perform. They want to succeed and close more deals just as much as management does and often salespeople want it more. However, since start-up sales is one of those jobs where the daily tasks are squishy, the proper compensation plan makes sure that the salesperson stays focused on what is important. The salesperson's drive for closing as many deals as possible in the shortest time span, is directly related to the compensation that she/he expects to receive. If your expectations are unrealistic, or comp plan too hard to calculate, you won't get the results you want.

When people ask me about building compensation plans, I typically recommend starting with a very simple plan so that it is easy for a salesperson to figure out what they will make with each sale.

When I needed my son to perform, I gave him two small goals: Get flags and get touchdowns. He went onto the field with those objectives in the forefront of his brain and his every move kept him on those two goals. In your business, you should find those small goals that your salespeople can achieve and have them attack it, and they should feel the immediate results - cash in the bank.

As the weeks progressed, I added incentives for other goals like proper blocking, passing, fair play, etc. and likewise, you can start to add other incentives around the goals that you need to achieve, but make sure that the goals you seek aren't too far out, and that they are achievable.

Recently, I spoke to the founder of a very early stage start-up with an enterprise sale where it will likely be several months before any sales are closed. The CEO was frustrated because he just didn't feel he had anything big to motivate his salespeople. It was clear that the salespeople would probably not make commission for 4-6 months because of the sales cycle plus the time lag of what it would take to get paid. I suggested he start by setting aside $5,000 in commissions. I told him to tell his two salespeople to go and get secured meetings with confirmed decision makers and have him pay $500 for each meeting to the salespeople. I also told him to clearly tell the salespeople that once the $5,000 was used up, it was used up. The result was that he spent the $5,000 in a little over a month and successfully kick-started his sales effort. It only cost him $5,000. He got motivated salespeople, and delivered a win-win.

The lesson here is that rather than just telling salespeople that they would make the money when they made the sale, he got into their heads, and gave them an incentive that matched the incentive of the company. Would the company have paid $5,000+ to get good leads elsewhere? Probably. So why not use it for sales motivation?

If it seems simple, that is because it is. Salespeople want to make money – and they will deliver in the easiest and fastest way for them to make money. Make sure your compensation plan allows salespeople to make money in ways that grow your business in the way you want it to grow.

(You can direct comments on my bad parenting to my QuotaCrush website – but when it comes to sales people, you can't argue with the logic)

HELP OR HURT

In my first start-up, like most start-ups, we were almost always cash starved. As a result of this, and also probably because of my sales-mind, we followed the following mantra to a tee:

*Everything that anyone does in a start-up boils down to one of two categories: Things that **help** sales and things that **hurt** sales.*

Whenever an employee was doing anything, they needed to consider if what they was doing fell into the first category or the second. If they decided it was the second, or couldn't find a clear indication that it was in the first category, then that employee needed to stop that activity and find an activity in the first category. Only once that person could not find ANY activity in the first category, should that person be working on an activity not clearly in the first category. No one should ever be working on any activity clearly in the second category.

I'm sure that many eyes are rolling, as they read this. "Ugh... typical sales guy who thinks he is the sun and the world revolves around him." But, the truth is that as severe and harsh and self-purposed it may seem, it is actually a very basic truth of every company that is cash-starved: You need to find ways to get the sales engine moving so that you are no longer cash starved. Once that is no longer the case, the world opens up.

Let's examine a very simplistic example. You own and are running a grocery store. A spill occurs and completely floods the entrance to the store. Would you, as the owner, not drop everything and make sure that people can come into the store? Of course you would. If people can't come into the store, they certainly cannot buy anything. If it meant that you couldn't get to the task of picking out the new aprons for the butcher that day, well then, that's OK.

What about re-stocking the shelves, or preparing the Sunday flyer? These should take precedence over activities like planning the company picnic, or next week's schedule.

When you look at a non-retail example, it gets a little greyer, but the concept is the same. Everyone should understand that if the web site is down, or not performing perfectly, or if the phones don't work, that should be fixed immediately. But what about your SEO (Search Engine Optimization) and editing your logo?

I have worked with start-ups, who allow their non-sales teams a great deal of latitude in what they work on and when, and this is a great attitude, but these people need to be coached on the essential nature of working on activities that help sales. If they are not helping sales, they are likely hurting sales. In one instance, I had a very large client on the hook for a license of some software, but we had a particular requirement that was critical to their acceptance of the product. It was something already on the development pipeline, but just not delivered yet. For about three weeks, the development team worked on some internal tools that they wanted in order to help them keep track of their goals, in lieu of working on the product development path that the client needed. The internal tools, while helpful to the team, were not in the critical path of what the client needed nor were we unable to function without them. The tech team just decided that it was what they wanted to work on in that time span.

This is a very bad practice. Every person on the team should have an interest in getting sales delivered and completed, and no task should ever take precedence or interrupt the critical path, whether that activity is in technology, operations, financial, legal or otherwise. Since the survival of the company is dependent on sales, everyone *should* care. Too often, sales people are viewed as "those overpaid pompous jerks" by non-salespeople in the company, which may or may not be the case. Regardless, even if they are overpaid and pompous, you still need people making sure that sales get done as quickly as possible.

When non-salespeople within your company are not prioritizing sales-related activities, they are, in effect, hurting the sales process even if they do not mean to do this. It is the business' job to make sure that everyone is working together to make sure that sales happen, get delivered, and customers experience joy and remain customers.

When I was in my first job out of Stevens Institute of Technology, I worked for a containerized shipping company, and wrote code for automating the shipping port. (In case you didn't read the introduction, I did start my career as a programmer, but quickly learned after I started my first company that I was significantly more talented in sales than I ever was with a compiler.) On the successful launch of our project, the CEO of the company came to the port to see the operation. While reviewing the smooth motion of the trucks thru the port, he saw a trucker changing a tire and struggling with a lug nut. The CEO made an off-hand comment, "you know...someone should fix that...there should be an easier way," and then he continued on his tour.

Some managers heard this comment, and proceeded on a six month engineering study of lug nuts, and eventually came back to the CEO with an entire plan on new and improved lug nuts, and what the implementation plan and costs would be to equip the entire fleet of chassis with new lug nuts. These new lug nuts would reduce the amount of stress on drivers needing to change tires. Needless to say, these managers were quite proud of the work they had done.

After the presentation of the lug nut plan, the CEO sat for a while before responding in anger, "What the hell is this?" When these managers explained that he had made a comment about the lug nuts and that someone should fix it, not only did the CEO not remember making the comment, he certainly did not appreciate the hundreds of thousands of dollars that were spent in a research study about how to make them better.

This story is always in the back of my mind. Why? As a salesperson, I'm always trying to make sure that I choose my words wisely – and I attempt to be mindful of everything I say. You can never be sure what small off-hand comment will be taken as gospel, or what small comment might offend or kill a deal. You certainly need to keep your online presence clean, which I'll talk about later on in the book, but what I'm talking about here is something even deeper. It's about making sure that you are careful in even the smallest things you say – not only because you might offend someone – but also because you might take the prospect in a direction you don't want them to go. Or you might get them thinking about issues that will cloud the deal and take longer for it to get done.

One time, an account manager and I were in a meeting, and before the presentation, all the people in the room were having a friendly chat about their smartphones. The account manager made a comment about how the wireless service on his phone was so bad he had been late to answer quite a few emails over the past few weeks. Harmless comment? Perhaps in some meetings, but this prospect focused on this comment throughout the sales presentation. He worried and obsessed about bad wireless service and wondered if this was going to affect the services we were trying to get him to purchase. (We were selling SMS marketing services). Instead of listening to the presentation as deeply as he should have, he was thinking about undelivered messages, failed expectations of customers, issues with marketing, and more. He needed to be convinced that this new way of marketing was going to deliver the experience his market expected, and now he spent most of the meeting focused on the negatives.

Simple comment about phones? Not so much. It was a manifestation of his basic fear about using our product.

Managers and entrepreneurs can take lessons from this as well. As a person in authority, you need to make sure that you are careful about how you phrase things and be clear in what you need your people to do. I've seen sales managers complain about sales metrics on call counts and cost per meeting. That resulted in salespeople taking their eye off the ball of closing deals in the pipeline and focus on increasing call counts. Having a constant desire to look good in the eyes of the boss, people will do what they think their boss wants them to do, just like in the lug nut example above. But that may often NOT be what the boss ultimately wants them to do. This is NOT a cheer for micro-management (I'm vehemently opposed to that), but it is a cheer for making sure you are careful in what you ask of your people, and that you continually check-in to make sure your employees are on-track.

I'm not sure what ever happened to those lug-nut designs and if they were ever acted upon, but I know the story has had a tremendous impact on my career and in the ways that I treat conversations.

THE RISK OF BEING DEAD RIGHT

In order to be a great salesperson and/or a great entrepreneur, you have to have conviction. You have to believe in your own vision and in your own ability to execute that vision if you expect to have any chance of success

When I was in my first start-up, I had a particular vision for my product and my company. I had a particular vision of the design of my software, and exactly how it would and should work. I had ideas about how it should be priced, and how it should be sold. As it turns out, I was wrong on nearly every one of those points to a particular degree. The great news is, as a salesperson at heart, making the necessary modifications to my thinking, my product, my pricing, etc., was not a hard chore for me. I found no shame in adapting my product and my company vision over what I learned from the marketplace.

As I engage with more and more non-sales minded entrepreneurs, I find it interesting in how these people think about the market, and how they should react to it.

It's great to have a vision and to believe you are going to change the world, but more often than not, you are going to be wrong. Whether or not you succeed is going to hinge very much on your ability to react and adapt to these things when you are wrong. More often than not, it's your sales team that will hand you the critical information to make the right decisions.

Yet I often see entrepreneurs sticking to their plan and vision, almost obstinately. This is extremely frustrating to the sales team and most certainly a recipe for failure. I call this syndrome *"dead-right."* When you are dead-wrong, it usually means that you are so incorrect in your thinking that it leads to your demise. *Dead-right* is exactly the same thing but you are so correct in your thinking that it leads to your demise. It means that while you may be 100% sure that your vision will change the world, and you may be 100% right that this is the way your product should work and be sold, you fail in the mean-time by not being able to react to your market. You may be right – but you will also die.

If you choose to stand by your convictions about how the product should function, be priced, and accepted by the world, the stars may align and you may win. But often, not being able to react and adapt to your market will cause you to fail. Ask yourself if you would rather be right about everything and fail or be flexible and survive long enough to realize your ultimate solution?

When I work with entrepreneurs, I can usually understand the vision, and typically see where it is that entrepreneur wants to go with the market. Once that is understood, the solution can be sold. Typically, entrepreneurs find that the market thinks about things differently. Entrepreneurs, who work with their sales teams and are willing to take slight detours along the path to success, usually find better adoption and growth. Sometimes it isn't even a deviation from product vision – but instead a reaction to HOW the product is sold.

For example, a while ago I had two clients I was working simultaneously. One was very market driven. The founder had a vision of where he wanted to go with his product and how he saw the world changing. We worked together closely, and with each sales win and sales loss, we adapted the product and pricing in ways that would make it more sellable, but wouldn't compromise too much on the ultimate direction. This entrepreneur was never at risk of being dead-right, and we never lost a sale due to this factor. We changed and adapted from a large ticket annual price, to a per-user fee, to a monthly all-you-can-eat model. We were flexible as we learned about the market, what people wanted for the product, and how they wanted to get it. This entrepreneur is now running a very profitable company.

The second entrepreneur was a very technical entrepreneur and looked at every sales problem as an engineering equation. He refused to bend in his thinking about how the product should be sold, and how it should be delivered. In a pure sense, his vision was correct. If his prospects bought into his vision from the start, they would have benefitted in the long run. But they just wouldn't do it. Despite this, I could not get him to compromise with me. He expected the prospects to bend to his will on command. For nearly 9 months, sales lagged, and the company struggled. Finally, in desperation, when it looked dire for the company and I was nearly ready to give up on him, he agreed to try some of my ideas. Suddenly we started making sales. The company is now doing very well and is back on its original trajectory toward delivering the solution in the way that they always wanted to deliver it.

The second entrepreneur came very, very close to being dead-right. How many don't make that last, desperate change, or leave enough runway to be able to make those changes? The entrepreneur and the sales team have to work together to find the ways that the product can sell, and get it sold. It's sad to see entrepreneurs that are SO close to success, but they just can't see it! They are so stuck on their idea of what should happen, that they couldn't get outside themselves to find out what the market needs. That is what the sales team is for - so use them for it.

I know naysayers will want to point out that people like Steve Jobs stuck to their vision regardless of what the customers told them and they were wildly successful. Yes, this is true in a handful of cases, but 99% of entrepreneurs out there are not Steve Jobs, Bill Gates, Steve Case, Mark Zuckerberg, or any of these exceptional people. There are many more stories about people who stuck to it and failed than those that stuck to it and won.

I would even argue that these exceptional people reacted to their markets as well in their path to success. Do you think Steve Jobs, in his ultimate vision, wanted to create an iTunes for Windows? Steve Jobs didn't want to have apps on the iPhone at all. Yet in both instances, he saw these as necessary deviations from his ultimate vision AS A PATH TO HIS ULTIMATE VISION. If you buy an iPod and connect it to Windows and see how great one Apple product is, maybe you'll buy a Mac when you replace your next PC. And guess what, thousands of people did just that. Steve Jobs reluctantly added apps to the iPhone, and now the app store is a massive revenue source for them AND why people stay locked into the ecosystem. So, even the great visionaries know that they need to deviate and react to their market in order to realize their ultimate vision.

So if you really, really believe you can bend the world to your desire and vision, then by all means risk being dead-right – but understand that it is a very big risk.

Better bet? Listen to your market, listen to your sales team and adapt.

STOP COUNTING CALLS

In an established company with an established product, you can count outbound calls, and you can require a minimum number of calls, because you have a defined product, a defined market, a defined price, and a well-defined pitch. When all of those are in place, then you can very easily dictate that it is simply a numbers game – and you can insist on driving as many calls as possible to get the required results. At some point, it will be well defined that x calls leads to y sales, but not when you start.

In a start-up, the dialing is about learning, so that you can get to the defined pitch, the defined price, the defined market and the defined product. If you force a number of calls, then it's possible you aren't listening enough and learning enough. Rather than using those calls to learn, you are just feeling good about driving thru a number of calls – for which you can pat yourself on the back and say "well at least I made 100 calls today". But who cares if you made 100 calls if you didn't learn anything about how to convert more of them? This is critical in a start-up. Start slow so that you can crush the numbers later on.

Clearly, you need to have every sales person dialing, but it's ridiculous to try to grab metrics around the number of calls in the initial phases when you still don't know if you have a repeatable sale. If it were my start-up and the sales person made four calls in a day, and came back with four very useful lessons about how, when, and for what amount, people would buy - but no sales, I would take that over someone that blasted through 100 leads and gave me one sale but no lessons.

As you get further along, you also need to take pause in using dialing metrics to judge salespeople. I worked in one situation where I had two salespeople who worked for me. One salesperson was a machine gun. He pounded through a lead list and dialed like mad until he made sales. The other person was an elephant hunter. He researched each and every client he was about to call and carefully prepared each pitch. The results were that, while the second guy made significantly fewer calls, the actual cash in the bank was nearly equal. Results are what matter in a start-up and really in any company. If a person makes 10,000 calls and no sales while another person makes ten calls and nine sales, which salesperson would you keep? If you answered the second guy, then ask yourself why you are focused so much on call metrics.

In a start-up, the best plan is to hire good people and let the comp plan and results dictate your metrics – not some arbitrary number of calls.

DO ANY OF YOUR METRICS MATTER

When you take this idea even further, you really need to take a hard look at what metrics you are collecting, why you are collecting them, and what they mean.

Metrics are used all over in sales organizations:

- How many calls did you make?
- How many connects did you make?
- How many meetings did you schedule?
- How many new leads did you add to the pipeline?
- What's the weighted pipeline?
- What's the percentage growth of the pipeline per week?

Metrics are how managers feel good about how people are doing. It is how they can point to things and say, "Look! My people are working." Often, it is how managers and CEO's can turn to their board and investors and say, "I have no idea how we didn't make our numbers this month, we made 4,000 outbound calls!"

You are in start-up mode. Here is the secret that no investor will ever tell you (likely because they don't understand this fact either): *None of it matters.* NONE. Should you track metrics? Yes, track them, but you should not manage to them. In a start-up or growth business, there is only one real metric that matters: **quota.** The bottom line metric for any and all salespeople is their quota. I don't need busy salespeople who don't close. Ask yourself again which salesperson you want on your team: the one who makes five calls a day and closes five deals? Or the one who makes his defined 60 calls a day but only closes two? If investors are asking you about metrics for your sales team, will any of it matter if you aren't bringing in revenue? If you are bringing in crazy amounts of revenue and have no metrics, how critical do you think they will be of how you are running the company and the sales process?

All too often, I see managers focus on the wrong metrics and force behavior that ultimately leads to less (or worse) sales. Especially in the start-up phase, you need sales conversations to be learning lessons so that you can get to the repeatable sale. It's certainly true that in a more established business with an established product that is well known by your prospects, you can draw a conclusion that x dials yields y dollars in sales. But this is rarely true in a start-up and in fact leads your salespeople to have the wrong behaviors.

In a start-up, you need to sell your value to your prospect. In order to sell value, you need to understand your prospect – their needs, their corporate goals, their issues, and their problems. This takes some research time. If you expect your salesperson to make 60 calls a day, guess how much research is done prior to making that call on their list. NONE! Oh, maybe a real quick Google search, but that is it. Essentially, your salesperson will dial each person blind. Therefore, most of those calls will be wasted.

Be informed about any personal connection with that client. Be informed about their corporate initiatives that match your product. Be informed about where the person being dialed fits into the organization.

Being armed with good information is key to making sales more quickly. Make sure that your salespeople are doing this. If you are a salesperson, do this.

And make sure the metrics that you are tracking don't get in the way of your selling.

PIPELINE CALLS

Salespeople work independently for the most part. Managers tell them what they need to do, and off they go and attempt to make sales. At some point, the team needs to get together and discuss the progress and share experiences.

Typically, pipeline calls will be held on Monday, and occasionally on Friday as well. Some sales managers hold pipeline calls daily or even at the beginning and end of each day. I personally think that is overkill, but some managers like it. My personal method is to have a pipeline call first thing on Monday morning (or mid-day if the team is spread across time zones). Occasionally, I would also have a Thursday or Friday call where the team would review learnings of the week.

Pipeline calls are very important, and they should not be missed. When I started my first company, I had no formal sales training, so my sales were haphazard, my tracking was minimal, and my team was tiny. While we had ad-hoc meetings about different clients, there was no structured weekly meeting. Sales certainly got done, and the entire team was often involved, but we didn't have anything formal. In many ways this was how we wanted to work. It was a free form and "make it happen" approach.

As the team grew, and the team became more dispersed, we instituted weekly pipeline calls to make sure that we all got on the phone at least once a week to discuss the challenges and the opportunities of the week prior, the week to come, and also to make sure we were all on target for quota. The calls were very productive, and became a team-building exercise. As each salesperson went through their deals, other salespeople would chime in and offer advice on how they handled a particular objection, or obstacle. The team would also share new points that would resonate as well as success stories that others could use in their prospecting and closing.

Once I saw the benefit to having a pipeline call, I could not believe that we functioned as a team without one. A sales manager should be talking to members of their team constantly. Especially when they are in the closing phases, managers should be aware of the challenges that each individual salesperson is having and assisting each in the way needed. Someone might be having problems with generating leads, another with research, and yet another with getting past gatekeepers. Pipeline calls do NOT replace any of the constant communication between manager and direct report, but they do reflect the one time the team is required to get together and discuss the entire sales effort and help each other.

It is extremely important to keep the purpose and the structure of the meeting positive and helpful. Otherwise, you aren't doing the team any benefit. In one of the sales jobs I had, there was a sales manager who was from the other side of the coin. On my first pipeline call after joining the team, I was asked to talk about the deals I was working on. I chimed in and started talking about a deal that I was enthusiastic about, but was having some problems with the value proposition. I started asking for advice from some other salespeople. The sales manager immediately stopped the conversation and said, "I hired you because you are a supposedly an expert in sales. If you can't figure this out on your own, then maybe I hired the wrong person." His idea of a sales pipeline call was a weekly bashing of every salesperson on their deals, not a constructive discussion on how to light a fire in the funnel of deals. He tried to find a way to embarrass each and every salesperson on the call and create an atmosphere where you were so nervous about getting yelled at that you didn't dare not have the answers to every question, and you wanted to make sure you had a close or two so that you would be closer to an "atta-boy" than you were to a verbal beating.

I went on to become the top salesperson, and we did have a very cohesive team, but that was something we built on the side. Salespeople would call each other and ask advice on different tactics that were working and not working, how one of us had gotten thru a logjam at a client, or how we found that incredible lead, etc. Members of the team had these discussions about deals outside of the sales pipeline call, and I'm sure lots of ideas were lost that the entire team could have benefitted from. I only heard about ideas that I called people about – or after we started talking on the side about some other topic. The "learning" portion of the pipeline call was lost – and I'll bet quite a few sales and salespeople in the process.

If you intend to run the second type of pipeline call, then I say that you should skip it. The weekly bashing of the salespeople and trying to embarrass them into performing is counter-productive and treating the team in such a manner certainly has little to no value.

The frequency of the pipeline call is really up to you and your particular needs. I personally think that anything more than two per week takes too much time away from selling. Salespeople won't listen as intently if it's every day; nor will they share as much since it will be so routine. They will just want it to end (salespeople don't like being forced to sit in one place for a long time). When I ran teams that had two calls, the first was the theme of, "What are we going to get done this week?" and the second was "What did we learn this week?"

Every salesperson should be coming to every pipeline call with a good knowledge of their pipeline, and be prepared to talk about each deal they are working on. In particular, they should be able to address what the next steps are, what the delay is (if any), when the deal should close, and **what they need from someone else**. The manager should be taking that last part away from the meeting.

THE SALES MANAGERS JOB

In the compensation section of the book, we discussed that you should never expect your sales manager to be both a coach and a player. Now let's go over exactly what the sales manager *should* be doing.

The sales manager's job is to be the over-arching guide of the sales process. In a start-up, this person may be the non-sales founder. No matter what, it is the job of the sales manager to watch over all the moving parts of the sales process and make sure that they happen.

A great sales manager starts her week with all the activities that surface on the pipeline call. After all, the ENTIRE pipeline is her responsibility, and the success and quota of the team are all on her shoulders. In a pipeline call, the sales manager should have collected all the information of what the team needs from other people within the organization, and also what each sales rep need the sales manager to do on their behalf.

The sales manager should be doing anything and everything towards moving the pipeline and sales effort forward including, but not limited to:

- Assistance in closing deals
- Working deals
- Pushing on marketing to get more leads

- Settling conflict among the team
- Pushing on other departments to get information or other items that they need to close deals
- Managing the pipeline
- Assigning leads and territories
- Evaluating staff (hiring/ firing /etc)
- Setting goal and evaluating compensation plans
- Tracking metrics and creating reports for management

The sales manager should be dividing their time among the sales reps to make sure that wherever there are problems, they are being solved. Sales reps are very proud people, and the manager needs to poke and prod to find the areas that may need help with a rep.

A great sales manager is a facilitator. She is someone who breaks the logjams internally and externally. She greases the pipeline and makes sales move more smoothly. She makes sure that her sales reps make a lot of money – because that's how she makes a lot of money and the company makes a lot of money. She does all of this by helping the sales staff in any and all ways possible to get deals done.

TERRITORIES

Once you have more than one sales person in your company, you will need to define territories so that you are fair about which sales rep gets to work on which leads. In the initial phases of a company, it will be hard to know which types of accounts are going to wind up being the best, the most profitable, or the easiest to close, etc. Setting territories can be very difficult.

Territories can be assigned on any basis you want. The most common approaches base territories according to geography or industry. But in a start-up, it's not uncommon to simply assign territories by the first letter of the company name, or in round-robin style as the leads come in. Sometimes, you may want to assign territories based on company size or revenue so that the more experienced reps handle bigger companies.

If you hoped this book would give you the magic formula for territories, I have to apologize, because unfortunately, one does not exist. It especially does not exist for nascent sales organizations. You really just need to make a best guess at what you think will fairly and equitably divide the companies that come in and give the reps and the company the best chance to close the most deals. And then be ready to shift and change as you learn.

Some other considerations when dealing with territories:

RE-ASSIGNING

You really want to be fair so that every rep has an equal chance at hitting quota. If you determine that a particular industry has no real value proposition, or one geographic area has very few customers, you have to determine what is best for the company so that the company as a whole has the best chance of closing as many deals as possible. You must monitor and try to determine if you have been fair in your assignments.

If you determine that you have been unfair, you must split the territory or change the territories. While the salesperson who has the plum territory may complain, splitting up a territory that has lots of low hanging fruit may be what has to be done in some situations. Whenever you decide to change or readjust territories, it will be a very unpleasant conversation for the person who is losing the territory, so you have to handle it delicately. Typically, I recommend that you handle the change in territory the following way:

- Any account already closed in the old territory the sales rep can keep as an account for some period of time, typically a year (unless of course the travel is massive and you are hiring a rep close by).

- Sales reps have the rest of the month/quarter/year to close any outstanding accounts in the territory they are giving up, otherwise those prospects become the ownership of the new territory owner.

- Any other considerations are negotiable but must be agreed upon by both sales reps.

The idea is to be fair on all sides so that you don't have any rep feeling like they are being treated unfairly. Unfair treatment is a surefire way to lose sales reps. Losing great ones is tough, and typically in an "I was robbed of money" situation like this, you will be losing great ones.

As a sales manager, you must be very strict about the territories you create and you must help defend them. If someone closes a deal or steals a lead in someone else's territory, that person cannot and should not be rewarded. In all of my management roles, I have told sales reps that anyone can close deals in any territory that they like, but I will pay commission and credit quota to the OWNER of that territory, so they should only close deals outside their territory if they are feeling charitable.

If you do not guard and defend the territories, then your sales reps will stomp on each other, try to grab each other's low-hanging fruit and create massive animosity among the team. Salespeople are highly competitive, and they work for commissions. It doesn't matter how much the team gels and how much salespeople like each other, they will do their best to get the most deals. Remember, that they all need to reach quota in order to make sure they have a job going forward.

There are situations, however, where you will want to allow reps to work on deals outside of their territory. For example, let's say that sales rep Paul's brother-in-law is a decision maker at WidgetCo and he has agreed to buy your product thru a discussion that Paul had at Sunday dinner. Or, perhaps Mary closed a big fish in one industry, but that decision maker moved to another company. Mary thinks she can close him again. Or, perhaps Mary has been very successful in an industry and there is a named account you feel very comfortable that she can close it quickly.

How do you deal with Fred whose territory is where this account sits? The first and best option is to actually let the reps work out an agreement between themselves that is equitable to each of them. When I ask reps to work it out, I typically offer a few suggestions about how I think they should do it, but then give them freedom to make a deal. The reps usually come up with some very fair ideas that make them both happy – and since you are hopefully fostering a great team mentality through your pipeline calls, they should be willing to work it out.

If, however, the reps cannot work it out alone, you have to stick to the territories firmly. The manager should try to offer suggestions and convince the reps to do what is best for the company. You have a few possibilities and you need to make sure you are fair about it.

Some equitable deals include:

- Simply swapping named accounts. If you give me WidgetCo in your region, I'll let you try to close TchotckeCo in my region.

- Mary gives Fred 25% of her commission for the right to close the deal, or even 50%.

- Fred gets the quota credit since it is his territory, but the commission goes to Mary who closed the deal.

Whatever the reps decide, or you decide for them, both parties should feel fairly treated, but the overriding rule must be that, when all else fails, territory assignments prevail.

MY TERRITORY MOVED ON ME

In very rare instances, the territory can change underneath the sales rep. In one sales situation, I was the NY-based sales rep for a company and was closing a large deal with a major network in New York. Everything was buttoned up and ready to be signed, and then the network let me know that internally they decided that the budgets

83

and the operations would run out of the parent company offices in California. The problem? California was another territory.

In this instance, my sales manager made the call and decided, correctly, that the account should stay with me since the entire sales effort was out of NY. The fact that the deployment was in LA was inconsequential to me.

Of course, I took a long time to close this deal and wanted to be able to close add-on business, which would now be in California so we had to decide how to handle it. The CA Rep and I decided that we would work together on add-on business and anything he closed in the next year, he would give me 25%, and anything I closed, I would give him 25%. It was a fair trade because I knew that I wouldn't be able to travel back and forth enough to close a lot of extra business and he was 5 miles from the customer. The end result was equitable for both of us.

If this situation happens for you, you need to look carefully at the situation and determine a way to make sure everyone is happy at the end of the result.

THE MURDER BOARD

The essential but horrible sounding tool called the murder board. Every time I bring it up with a new person, I get confused stares – yet it's an essential tool for both salespeople and entrepreneurs.

What exactly is a murder board? Murder Board is a term that was originally coined by the U.S. military and referred to the practice of preparing people for oral exams; particularly for oral exams related to becoming an instructor. A panel of several people would be convened to hear the presentation of the candidate, and to become the worst set of students that this instructor would ever face. They wanted to see how they would handle the frustration, humiliation, and the general situation. The thought process was that if they could handle that panel of people, then there would be no student that could topple them. At the end of the "murder board," the instructor would get a thumb up or down. If they received a thumb down, they would be subjected to *another* murder board. This ritual was part training and part hazing, but actually probably quite effective at weeding out bad instructors and preparing the good ones.

So what does this have to do with sales and entrepreneurship? When we talk about murder board as it relates to sales, it is not a hazing technique, but rather an essential tool to arm the salesperson with responses to all of the tough questions that a customer can ask. It has the same roots, but can truly be critical in making sure that you don't blow that meeting that you worked so hard to get.

I recommend murder boarding early and often. It is very easy in the early stages of a company, or in a tight knit sales team to get into *group think* where you start to actually believe everything that you say in your pitch about your product, without taking a very hard and critical look at it with outside eyes.

A murder board should be conducted with one person taking the role of salesperson, and the other people taking the role of hypercritical clients that have a problem with anything and everything. This should NOT be a hazing experiment to see if you can throw this person off their game just for the fun of it, but it should be difficult. The point is to prepare yourself, to learn about your product, and to get better and better pitches (and perhaps learn something more about your product in relation to your competition and the world in general. The people serving as the clients need to object to any and every part of the product and pitch that is presented:

- I already use one of your competitors.
- It's too much money.
- That claim can't be true.
- My company already has a solution like that.
- I don't need this.
- Your type of solutions will never get past my senior management. We NEVER buy solutions like yours. It's against policy.
- I have more important priorities.
- This is a "nice to have."
- Your competition is cheaper.

- Etc.

If you have heard the argument, or think about the argument, you should bring it up. The person in the line of fire should be able to respond to each and every question in a proper way. Don't be afraid to get specific about your product and its features – because your potential customers won't.

When you stump the person presenting, you should stop and think about the question. Why did that particular objection or response throw you? Is it an overlooked product feature? Or a place where your competition trumps you? Or, is it just something for which you haven't thought of a proper response? Don't worry if you get stumped! **THIS IS GOOD!** It means you are learning something about your product, your pitch, or your ability to pitch. Work on and practice better responses to each objection and incorporate them into the arsenal you use in your selling.

The sales team should take turns on this, and iterate the pitch over and over again.

How often should you murder board? Often. Especially in the early stages of a product. It should help bring out deficiencies in the product and how to deal with them in the sales pitch. If you get a new objection in the field or lose a sale, bring it back into the next murder board and use the experience to determine if there are better ways to handle the objection, or deal with the competitive threat.

Murder board when you get new salespeople. Don't subject them first, but let them be the "bad client" first. Chances are their outside view will bring up something you haven't dealt with before and help the experienced people pitch better. Once they have heard the pitch a few times, they can role play themselves and have the experience of battling overly critical prospects.

I'm not sure how I would get better or how to train my teams better without the murder board, yet I'm always amazed when people in sales and start-ups say that they aren't murder boarding. Sure, there are a lot of people claiming to role-play, but that is not completely the same thing. In role-play, there is not necessarily a concentration on raising all the possible objections. So, make sure you murder board often.

SCRAPPY VS CHEAP

Start-ups need to save cash whenever they can. However, you have to be very careful not to fall down the "cheap" route, especially when it comes to sales efforts. Being scrappy is okay, but being cheap is not.

For example, at one start-up, we really couldn't afford the high priced ticket to a premier event in our industry. So, what we did instead was to go to the city, got a room in the hotel, and setup meetings with prospects outside the event. They were all going to be there, so it made sense. When we didn't have meetings, we congregated in the lobby of the hotel (we were guests so that was okay), and struck up conversations with anyone we could, just as if we were in the event. Scrappy? Yes. We didn't get to exhibit so we didn't get the benefit of that foot traffic, and we didn't get to see the attendee list and all the other benefits of attending the event, but we were scrappy about trying to make sales.

Another start-up that I went to decided that in order to save money, they only purchased one license to the CRM (Customer Relationship Management) software, and the office manager was in charge of updating the data based on emails that would go back and forth between her and the sales reps. I immediately stopped that disaster and got each sales rep their own login to the CRM. This company was saving a few thousand dollars a year, but was nearly eliminating the effectiveness of the CRM. In fact, no one was really tracking anything. This was an attempt to be scrappy, but was really just being cheap. Tools are needed by sales people to be effective.

SUMMARY

Building out a sales team and a sales process is very difficult. I would even say that this is a bigger and more difficult task than actually building your product itself. Attracting salespeople in a start-up is difficult enough, but then maintaining them and keeping them interested becomes yet another set of challenges.

Unless you have carried a bag yourself and understanding how difficult this life is, you will always be behind the ball in terms of knowing what it truly feels like to be that person who is living and dying by that sale – to live every day with a target on your head.

But business owners who have not been salespeople need to take the time to understand what the sales process is all about. They need to try their best to support and nurture their sales team, its process, and get inside their heads, have the best chance to succeed.

This entire section is your friend, and you should refer to it often as you experiment with pricing, compensation, and finding the right people to be on your team.

SELLING FOR A START-UP

The next and more important challenge at any start-up is actually getting someone to buy your product. To be perfectly clear, this is actually required in every company. It doesn't matter if you are selling data exhaust from your free service, advertising space on your web site, or charging the people who directly use your product or service; you have sales in your company.

Some of the advice about how to sell when you are working in a start-up is just normal sales – what works there will work everywhere. But, when you sell for a start-up, everything is magnified – fears about your company, your product, your claims, your sustainability, your competition, and more. So, it's especially important for you to be sensitive to your prospects, and understand what their challenges are in buying from you, and you need to work harder than most to get the sale done.

In this section of the book, the topics covered will explore both basic sales advice and some very specific sales advice all tailored for success in a start-up.

A few years ago, I went on a sales call with an important client. It was actually a six-month review on all the work that we had done for the client, in hopes of gaining more business with the client. I brought with me one of the senior analysts at the business, who was set to explain the details of the majority of the results that we were going to be presenting at the meeting.

We all sat down in the room, and I got up in front of the room and began the meeting. "Thank you for inviting us in today. We are very pleased with the outcome of all the work we have been doing together over the last several months, and we hope you will be pleased too. We are going to start..." I said.

"Excuse me," interrupted the most senior person in the room at the client's office, "are you a salesperson?" "Yes," I replied. "Okay, then please stop talking and let HER talk," she said motioning to the senior analyst I brought with me. "I hate salespeople... no offense."

Unfortunately, this is the reputation that salespeople have. Sales people are meant to separate you from your money and convince you that you need things that you might not need. The truth becomes hazy and you often feel taken advantage of.

The world is filled with these types of salespeople, and there are countless books written on how to become a ruthless salesperson, yet if you look at many of the most successful salespeople, they are not like this. They are good PEOPLE. This is what makes them good salespeople.

I'm not arguing that you can't make a lot of money and succeed if you take the route of being a ruthless salesperson, but I will say that you will have an easier time building your start-up from scratch if you take the advice of being better people first.

You should actually care about your customers and their problems – and look to solve them. It will help you build rabid fans that will cement your foundation for future sales. Swindle or cheat your first few customers? You probably will not be in business for long.

Want to be a better sales person? Be a better person.

NO ROOM FOR PRIMA DONNAS IN A STARTUP

If you want to sell at a start-up, be prepared for extra work.

It is unlikely that your start-up will have someone in marketing to help you build your presentations. That will be on you. Lead generation will probably be mostly up to you. If you need a proposal or RFI (Request For Information) drawn up, you will probably create it yourself. Editing images for sales collateral? You are likely on your own. Need your outside lawyer to review the contract? Go talk to the General Council of the company to get it done... oh wait... we don't have one of those. Need flights booked for that tradeshow? Open your own browser and search. Booking a dinner for your important clients? Call around and find a table yourself.

You have a lot of opportunity at a start-up, but it comes with a cost. There will not be sales infrastructure for you – and you are going to shoulder the burden of this. Companies should and often will, help out in any way that they can, but closing deals is on you, and you cannot let the lack of infrastructure stop you from getting deals done.

And the most important thing is to never whine about it and never be a prima donna about having to do things that are "not your job."

Having always worked at small, struggling companies, I have always worked in environments where everyone did three jobs because the money just wasn't there to hire everyone we needed in order to get things done. In these companies, there is rarely the correct infrastructure, or structure to have a sales person just walk over with a signed order and place it in a wire basket and know that it is going to get done.

At one company in particular where I worked as a sales rep, there was NO structure in how to get a sale through the company. I worked in New York running the northeast and the company was in Atlanta. I was working on some massive deals with multiple major corporations. When I started working on these deals, I was thrilled to have gotten us in the door and through the initial screen. Now, these large companies were seriously considering us for their business. However, these guys typically work with other companies of their size and stature and what irritates them about working with small companies is the lack of structure and process. So, a sales person needs to make sure that the large company gets the customer's process followed whatever it may be and there may not be someone in your company that is going to do this.

I would very often get on a plane down to HQ and essentially walk the RFP (Request for Proposal), contract, etc., from desk to desk and stand behind people until they did what I needed them to do. If I didn't fly down, I would be on video chat, the phone, texting, etc., until I got what I needed. I was never nasty about it, and people were generous with their time and information. I always understood that they were busy, and my commission was not the most important thing to them.

Did I like the fact that I had to do all of this? No. Did I like occasionally having to do other people's jobs for them so that it got done? No. But, there is NO place in a growing company for a prima donna salesperson. If you want the commission, then get off your butt and help the sale all the way through. If you sell software, go do the installs. If you sell high-end landscaping items like trees and bushes, then put on some gloves and pick up a shovel.

A good excuse for not getting a sale is still just that - an excuse.

FIND A MENTOR

One day, I got a call from my mentor. He happened to be in the city, had a few hours between meetings, and wanted to grab a cup of coffee. As luck would have it, I was not too busy, and I made the time to go sit down with him. The experience was so energizing that it reminded me just how valuable having a mentor can be for a salesperson.

My mentor is someone that I actually hired into the first company that I founded. His role was to help me rebuild sales for our company post-9/11. I didn't think that we needed to hire anyone, but the venture capitalists insisted that we do an executive search and find someone with serious turn-around experience to ensure that we would have success. He and I instantly hit it off, and quickly we were making huge sales strides working on the accounts together.

Until that time, I had been doing, in my eyes, very well in sales without any formal training. I also had been cultivating the accounts for years, and didn't think I needed anyone to help me push them over the finish line. It's likely that I could have made most of the sales alone, but am I EVER grateful that the venture capitalists insisted on that hire. The amount of REAL sales knowledge that I have gained through his insight is something that I never could have gained had I just figured it out as I went along – as I had been.

The story is that I believe I am a natural salesperson. I was able to sell my company idea to investors. I was able to sell my product, from my small start-up, to huge corporations that based mission critical projects on it: core delivery business, year 2000 migrations, etc. However, my sales technique and strategy were never toned. Once I melded my mind with the processes of a true professional lifetime salesperson, I was able to accelerate and understand how to crush sales.

I email, talk, or meet with my mentor several times a year – and it is always very refreshing to get his perspective on the current challenges I am facing. I also get to hear about his sales challenges and then we brainstorm together. He will take my call anytime and vice-versa. I'm always happy to hear about different views on different sales techniques and strategies. I welcome any guidance or advice he can offer up. Since he is constantly learning, too, the conversations are never old.

Salespeople, almost by definition, are very self-confident egomaniacs. You nearly have to be in order to deal with constant rejection, determine ways to overcome it, and/or move on from it. But because of self-assuredness, it can be very difficult for a salesperson to step out of this mindset and listen to those that may know more than they do. If you do not have a mentor, GET ONE. Better yet? Get a couple. Co-workers, former bosses, current bosses, or relatives. In fact, anyone with more or similar experience than you can be a mentor.

My entire career has been about start-up sales. Over time, I've learned quite a bit about how to make sales happen. In particular, I've learned a lot about how NOT to do something, and also how to read situations well so that I can come to win-win solutions.

Sometimes, I've learned these lessons through failing and picking myself up again. Other times, I've learned from talking to people more experienced than me. As I just mentioned, my sales mentor has been an incredible resource to me.

Yet other times, I've learned from watching the people who sell FOR me, or around me. I've seen younger, less experienced sales people have bursts of brilliance in sales and close or move deals with tactics that didn't come to me immediately. And, sometimes they may read a situation better than I have – and therefore have better insight in what the next move is.

Sales can be an art form, and it's hard to get it perfect every time. Fortunately, there are a lot of ways to learn and get better. I'm ALWAYS looking for new ways to get better at sales. When I discuss sales tactics with anyone…regardless of the level of experience of the person I am talking to, I would never discount what they are telling me about an account, in case there is something that I have missed, or perhaps there is an innovative way to move an account forward.

This is why it boggles my mind when fresh, young salespeople are SO arrogant that they refuse to listen to advice on how to get better at sales. It's easy to misread an account, miss a "closing" cue, commit sales self-sabotage, and more. The people around you: your mentor, your sales manager, other salespeople in your company, your CEO, and anyone else in and around your deal can offer you tips and cues to get better and you should be taking this advice.

I'm not perfect in my sales record. There isn't a perfect person out there. (If there is someone with a 100% close rate – then stop reading this book and go read his or hers!) However, there is nothing more frustrating than to see a young salesperson make blatant errors and then actually refute advice given to them by their sales manager and sales peers within the same company (they may have better sales track records). Just like me, you aren't perfect, and in fact, you haven't lived every possible scenario, so you don't have the perfect and complete arsenal of ways to overcome every situation. EVERYONE should listen more and learn more – and rarely should advice be refuted on first glance.

In my career right now, I'm often the master – but often I'm still the grasshopper. And, I'm okay with that. I want to learn and learn and learn so that I can continue to be a better master when I am called to be the master. I actually think that because I like to be the grasshopper, it makes me a better master when I'm called to be the master.

Be the grasshopper sometimes. It will serve you well.

DO THE RIGHT THING & SALES WILL FOLLOW

With a blog named QuotaCrush, you would think that my opinion is that salespeople and sales managers should be singularly focused on quota. In fact, that is completely counter to my entire belief system in terms of the best way to accelerate sales at a start-up.

Wait. Didn't I say in the section on metrics that the only metric that matters is quota? Yes I did. In terms of measurement of success, quota is the only measure that matters; however, in how you conduct sales, quota should not be your main or only concern.

The strategies I preach do, in fact, lead to more sales, but as you should notice in what is presented in this book, the bottom line is about finding and pursuing the right solution(s) for your prospects and clients. When you focus on the right solutions for your prospects and clients, reaching and ultimately crushing your quota becomes easy. And by continuing to do the right thing consistently crushing quota becomes possible. Trust goes a long way. The goal of a salesperson should be that people buy from you because of who you are. Prospects and clients should feel that the fact that you are talking about and pitching this product means that you believe in it. They should trust that you wouldn't sell them junk. When you have that type of reputation preceding you, then you have eliminated some of the largest obstacles in the sales process.

I don't consider myself to be "slick" in my sales approach. I would never sell something to someone if I didn't believe that what I was trying to deliver wasn't a solution to his or her problem. That's not to say that everything I've ever sold has worked out perfectly for the customer, but I never went into the sale believing there would be problems. And I have never tried to convince the customer to buy something they didn't need. And in the situations that the product hasn't worked out for the customer, I've always made steps to make it right.

During the times when it has been challenging to get sales done, I have often had to make major concessions and resort to creative pricing techniques in order to get sales over the finish line. But finding the right solutions is beneficial to both parties. I believe that these clients will receive tremendous value over the long run.

Someone joked to me recently that the state of the economy didn't matter, that somehow I could figure out how to get people to buy things no matter what. It is true that in an up economy and in a down economy, there are ways to make sales. In my circles, though, it's not the slick sales approach that allows this to happen – but the salespeople that understand the macro-environment, and work to find a solution that makes sense for all parties involved. When this happens, people feel comfortable buying.

When you do the right thing and when you are honest, sales happen for you. And the more honest you are, the more good karma comes back and leads to more sales.

SALES LESSON FROM A 7 YEAR OLD: HUMILITY

I look for sales lessons in everyday life. One time, I was treated to a very nice sales lesson from my seven-year-old daughter.

My wife called me and asked me how long it would be before I got home from work. That night, Erin, my seven-year-old daughter had to go to the PTA board meeting in town and my wife wanted to know if I could watch the other two kids, while she took Erin there. I wasn't going to make it home in time, but determined that if we met each other at the school, we would arrive just as the meeting would start. We could meet there, I would be available to assist in watching my other children, Erin could do what she needed to do, and then we could all grab a quick dinner.

When I arrived, I saw the father of one of Erin's best friends, and I started chatting with him. He said, "I see Erin was one of the finalists, too. Isn't that great?" It turns out that, in order to teach the kids about the presidential election that year, the school had put together a mock election. Each student was required to put together a platform for what should be the official healthy snack food for the entire school. Each student wrote an essay, and then it went through an entire election process, gaining electorate votes, etc. The top students in the school were asked to present their platform at the board meeting. My daughter and her best friend were among the top finalists.

Afterward, I asked my daughter about the selection process. When I told her what an amazing feat this was for her, she was surprised that I was so proud of her. It never occurred to her that this was a big deal. It just was what it was.

I am telling this story not to gush about my daughter (okay, maybe a little), but to illustrate something amazing about kids that we often forget about – and something critical to good sales people: **humility and the just do it attitude**. My daughter didn't think about failure. She didn't think about self-glory. She only did what she was supposed to do, and she did it to the best of her ability. Because she didn't really worry about failure, she wound up performing well above all of her peers.

She went out and just DID IT. When we as salespeople create imaginary obstacles in front of ourselves, we can lose before we win. We have to just go out there and try our best, and not worry about rejection, and not worry about losing deals; we need to just go for it.

Exhibiting humility, more importantly, is something that is essential to being a good salesperson. No one wants to deal with a cocky or pushy salesperson. Your amazing feats will speak for themselves, and the customers themselves will be your badges of honor. Think about how much MORE proud I was of my daughter because she didn't (and hasn't since) gloated about her honor.

RESEARCH

Great salespeople do research. People buy from people, and the more you make a personal connection with a person, the better chance you have of getting them to like you and buy from you. You also need to research so that you can find where their pain is and where they will find value from what you deliver.

There is no such thing as doing too little amount of research. The Internet has provided a wealth of information like never before in history. It's up to salespeople to find that research and use it to the biggest benefit.

You should research all of the following on the company and more:

- **Corporate Structure**: You should know about any divisions, parent companies, spin-offs, strategic alliances, etc.
- **Annual Reports**: If the company is public, you should be looking into what the CEO and Chairman have made as their corporate goals for this year and perhaps longer. Is there a way that you can make your prospect a hero in that corporate mission – and also that your product won't be counter to any goals (i.e. you sell printers and the corporate mission is to reduce paper)
- **Org Chart**: Do you know where your prospect fits into the organizational chart?
- **Press Releases/Articles**: In a similar fashion to the annual reports, you should be looking at any press releases from the companies and their partners to see if there are symbiotic or conflicting issues and be building a pitch around this.
- **News Stories**: Knowing any news that has come out on the company before a pitch is critical. Without this, you can easy make a gaffe that is unintended – or look as if you don't care about their problems. Even worse is missing out on an opportunity to solve a crisis because you were not aware.

- **Corporate Social Presence:** What are they tweeting? What is on their LinkedIn & Facebook pages? What are people saying about them on blogs? What does their CEO tweet about?

You should also research all of the people you are directly dealing with (or want to deal with), not only to find out about them, but specifically to find any "sparks" or connections between you that will allow you to have a more comfortable exchange or even get in the door.

On the individual, you should at *least* be researching in the following places and finding out whatever you can about them, what they like, where they hang-out, what their interests are, and more so you can find connections:

- Google their name: If you do not do a web search on each and every person that you call as a minimum research effort, then you will never become great, yet it is amazing how many sales people skip this step.
- LinkedIn profile: Where did they go to school? What sports did they play? To which fraternity or sorority are they a member? How are we connected? Where else have they worked and what types of positions have they held?
- Facebook page (if public): What brands and other items have they "liked"? How are we connected? What have they listed as hobbies / favorite authors, etc.?
- Amazon: What is on their reading list? What is on their wish list?
- Crunchbase/Wikipedia: What is the crowd saying about them? What other accomplishments do they have?
- Corporate bio (if available): What does the company list them as? How does the company position them?
- Twitter: What are they tweeting about? What do they like?
- Pinterest: What types of pictures do they post? Can you infer an interest from this information?
- Google news, their blog, and on and on

The more you want the deal, the more you should be researching. It is often hard to do this on inbound calls, but if you can, do it. On outbound calls, there is no reason to not do this.

Is it hard? Not particularly. Is it tedious? Yes. Is it rife with distractions that you must resist? Yes.

Is it essential? YES!

Once you have started the research you need to find the personal connections, both topical and current when you make the calls. For example, maybe you both played lacrosse in college. Perhaps you are both members of Delta Tau Delta. Perhaps you both tweet about high-tech. Perhaps you notice that her husband and your boyfriend are both Yankee fans. Whatever the connection, these are great ways to break the ice and make a personal connection.

I am not advocating stalking anyone, or going too far so as to be creepy. I know one time, I was being courted by a salesperson, and, on our first call, he said, "How is Theresa?" I didn't know this person, and it confused me because all of a sudden I wasn't sure how he knew my wife. After I stammered a little, I asked how he knew my wife. He explained that there was a profile that was written about my success in my first start-up that was posted on my university website and in it, it mentioned my wife's name. I commend this salesperson for doing his homework. He probably went to my LinkedIn page, saw that I went to Stevens Institute of Technology, then went to that page and searched on me to find the article and read it. Tremendous research chops and he learned quite a bit about me, but using an obscure piece of information to show he did this research gave me the creeps more than it warmed me up. Had he simply mentioned that he liked the article on me and asked a question or two about it, it would not have been creepy at all. So, certainly be sure that you are using any information that you find out in the right way.

Essential information that you research before a call can be simple as well. For example, it's critical to know what time zone you are calling so you don't catch somebody in the middle of lunch, but also nice to know about local happenings when you call. If the town you are calling recently had a tragedy, it's nice to address it: "I hope you weren't affected by X" rather than simply pretend it didn't happen. Creating any type of understanding makes you much more likely to appear empathetic to the problems they have – and hopefully you solve.

Without research, you put yourself at a major disadvantage in the sales and pitching process. Can you make sales without the research? Of course. But many times sales are won in the margins, with a razor thin difference between you and your competitor. Any and all boosts that you can give yourself actually matter.

As I mentioned, obtaining this information is critical, but tedious and rife with distractions, but there are plenty of great information tools which allow you to get at this information quickly, distraction-free, and allow you to focus on selling and closing more. (Full Disclosure: I founded and run a sales research software company called FunnelFire).

Research is also very helpful to aid in the sometimes-long pauses throughout the sales cycle. Over the course of my career, I have calculated that it takes my sales teams, on average 7 to 10 touches before they get a sale. What do you do to reach back out to that prospect? You can simply send an email, "Hey are you ready to buy my stuff today?" Or, you can send a thoughtful email with an article about the industry. Or you can congratulate the prospect on a press release. Or you can see a news story about the company and offer a thoughtful response as to how your company's products could be helpful.

When you connect with your prospect in this way, you become less of a nudge and more of a confident and a thought leader. That is the type of salesperson that people gravitate towards. Need to wake up an account? Reach out with something other than, "Are you ready to buy?"

Overall, you can see that research is a very, very critical part of your every day activities in sales, and the best salespeople spend up to 25% of their time doing it. Perhaps that is why they are the best salespeople.

When you sell for a start-up, all of your claims are questioned much more heavily than in an established company with a known reputation. Therefore, transparency and honesty in the sales process become that much more critical. When you do the right thing by your prospects and when you are honest, sales happen for you. And, the more honest you are, the more good karma comes back and leads to more sales.

A few years ago, I took a customer out to lunch since I was traveling in his city. This customer had been up on one of the software services for one my clients for about a month, and this was a great opportunity to get some feedback on the product, and talk about the implementation thus far.

At one point in the conversation, I paused and said to the customer, "So, how truthful was I in the sales process about what your post sales experience with our software would be?" He immediately replied, "Actually... very! You made some pretty bold statements in your sales process about what you guys could accomplish and I admit that I discounted some of what you said, but I'm certainly very pleased that you have come through on everything that you have promised."

Bold statements – but honest ones. If you put a value statement out there, and you back it up later on, it works wonders for you in the sales process.

This particular customer gave a keynote a few weeks later and raved about our product and implementation, and it led to quite a few additional sales for me. When I was selling for another client, he bought from me again – and the sales process was much quicker. When he bought from me a third time at another customer, I did it in a single sales call because he knew that anything I said, claimed, and promised would be the truth. By being honest with this customer, I now had a champion – and that means the world in the sales process.

It does happen sometimes, however, that a customer's experience is not exactly what they expected, and they may feel that you were not 100% true to your word. At these times, you need to make sure that the customer understands where your process may have failed, or fallen down. Perhaps you got new information after the sale that you didn't take into account before the sale, or perhaps external factors affected your ability to deliver. What you must do at this point is explain, in very truthful statements, what happened and map it back to those bold statements you made in the sales process. Presuming that the sales process had honest statements, you should be able to easily explain why the experience wasn't exactly what they thought it might be, and how you plan to get them back on track. Your open and honest communications here should be the way to maintain the relationship – and eventually get a champion again.

SOMETIMES WHEN YOU LOSE, YOU ACTUALLY WIN

I've often found that customers for whom you've had a failure, been honest about it, and then turn around, become even bigger champions. These customers know that they can trust your word completely. Problems happen to everyone and every account. It's how you deal with them that makes the difference.

At a company I was selling for, we had a MASSIVE mistake for one customer. It was an information technology failure on our part, and a very massive mistake. I found out about it, and immediately went to the CFO's office in person, sat down and told him of the problem and what we were going to do about it. I then sat there as he proceeded to scream at me for several minutes asking how we could be so stupid.

After the smoke stopped pouring out of his ears and his face resumed a normal color, he looked at me and said, "Well, you could have easily hidden this problem from me, so I have to respect you for being honest and for coming and telling me in person. That's probably the only reason I'll give you a chance to fix this." We did fix it, and the trust I gained from that customer was immense. From that point on, he knew there was no reason for him to doubt my word or think that I wouldn't be honest with him. I did quite a bit of additional business with that customer (including selling to him on my next sales gig).

When dealing with a person who makes money from commissions, the natural instinct of most people is to think that the salesperson is saying and doing anything to get the sale. Therefore, distrust is the natural emotion of the buyer. When you turn that on its head, you will be amazed at how much it will help in the sales process

CONTROLLED MESSAGING

Recently, I spoke to someone who had followed my advice about being **completely truthful in the sales process**, and was finding that he wasn't getting as many sales from it as he thought. I started digging into his process, and instantly realized the problem.

Truthfulness does not mean "reveal everything at once." Nor does it mean that you don't control what information you give at any time. You need truth in every step of the process, but that doesn't mean that you have to show your entire hand from the get-go. You should be offering up information in snack-sizes and when it is required to move the process along. You should always be managing the process towards the end goal that you want – a close.

Think of it this way… Go back to your single days (or if you are single, go back to last weekend), and imagine yourself in a bar and seeing an attractive person. You certainly don't walk up to them and say, "I just saw you, had a mental fantasy about us together, and thought I would come over here and talk to you. I think we are likely quite compatible and would make very attractive children. I have a marriage certificate here and a list of potential places where we could live."

While this may be a very truthful comment about your intentions, it reveals WAY too much information at once and reveals your ultimate goal without getting any feedback, or easing into the "sale"

What should you say? Probably something closer to, "Hi, can I buy you a drink?"

When you ask that, the person most likely KNOWS that you find them attractive. They probably KNOW you are trying to get closer to them to potentially find out if there are any "next steps" to the relationship, but it's WAY less threatening than the first approach.

As your relationship develops, *if* it develops, you can reveal the other information at appropriate points so that ultimately, you both wind up in the same place and live happily ever after with your attractive children.

Sales strategy is exactly the same. First, you need to understand your end goal and then you need to map out your process to get there. You need to then think about how your prospect sees the world and what things are important to them.

The overly truthful salesperson was cold calling, traversing the organization to get to the right person, and striking out most of the time. The problem was that he was revealing everything he planned on pushing to the people for whom he needed an introduction. The call went something like this, "Hi, Fred. Can you introduce me to Mary, your CFO? I'm going to try to sell her our product. You guys are a great organization and a great candidate for our enterprise package." While that was definitely truthful, it was also scary. He essentially asked for an introduction and revealed that he was going to be a pushy salesperson. Who wants to pass on that referral!? What should his call have been? "Hi Fred, I was hoping you could help me get an introduction to Mary, your CFO. My company sells a very interesting solution that may have applicability for her, and I'd like to set up an exploratory call with her to discuss." Fred should know from this conversation that Mary is going to get a sales pitch. That was obvious, but nothing was revealed about the fact that the enterprise product would be pushed.

Changing to this strategy yielded much better results for my friend.

START WITH THE RIGHT RELATIONSHIP

In one two-day span, I got calls from two of the banks that I do business with. The first one holds my home equity line, and I got a call from a woman who wanted to talk to me about my line. The second bank holds both my personal checking account as well as my business account.

What was interesting is that both banks were calling me with essentially the same exact pitch. Both women that called me wanted to call to establish a "relationship" with me. They wanted to let me know that they would be my "personal banker" and that I could call them with any questions and concerns and they would help me out.

I suppose that the banking industry is hurting for good customers now, and this is the effort that they are putting out there to try to establish the relationships that they should have been cultivating LONG before now – but that is not what this story is about.

I decided to entertain both of the calls because I found it interesting and I wanted to find out what they were offering. Neither woman could articulate what the added benefit would be for me with them as my "personal banker." They could set-up accounts for me, track down payments, and more. When I said that I was already doing everything they were talking about by myself online, without any interaction or problems, they still could not tell me why I should care that I now had a personal banker. Clearly, defining a value proposition should have been something that was in their pitch to me.

In reality, they are trying to establish a relationship with me because the entire banking experience has become very disconnected. I can get money from a machine and I do all of my banking on-line. In fact, I can't remember the last time I went to a bank and went through the second set of doors – I typically stop at the ATM and don't go further. As a result, I don't really care who my bank is or where they are located. I only care that they are solvent and that they make things simple and easy for me. I would switch banks / mortgages / etc., tomorrow if I found a better deal.

The banks are reaching out to establish a relationship that will make me more connected to the bank, and less likely to leave. They can step in and fix problems, and make me a happier customer. Today, I call a general 800 number and I am placed in a queue. Perhaps tomorrow I could call one of these women and have personal attention. (As an aside, one of the women spoke in broken English which was not very convincing that I would have an easier time). Both called me from branches close to my house, and explained that I could come in any time and talk to them about any issues I would have. Other than this, I could not figure out what the benefit would be to me – and really I am not looking for this in my bank.

As a credit to both banks, and why I've been with both of them so long, is because I have not had many issues calling the 800 number and getting my problems solved. But, honestly, I would leave both in a minute if they started to charge me fees, or make my banking experience more difficult. I moved to this bank 5 years ago because my last bank decided to add a $3 per month fee to on-line banking. It took me about an hour to move all of my business over to the new bank, switch over Quicken, and start banking somewhere new.

That was a long pre-amble to the point that I wanted to make - when you make a sale and get a new customer, you should be thinking about the relationship that you want to have from the beginning, not once you are into it. By making sure that you establish the right relationship from the beginning, you are more likely to have a customer for life. You will get the feedback that you want BEFORE you hear that they have cancelled your service.

In the 21st century, social networking platforms offer us lots of ways to establish great on-going relationships with our customers, and we need to use these tools to their fullest to make sure that we are engaging our customer base and making sure that they feel part of the solution and not just a number.

It's possible that it's not too late for the banks to establish a relationship with me and prove to me that they can offer me value that another bank cannot. But, as you can see, I got the same pitch from two different banks within a week. I'm not sure that this pitch is going to sway me one way or another at this point. It makes me think that all banks will offer the same product. Had the initial interaction with a bank been one that made my life so much easier and convinced me that they would be there for me – then I would have been better sold and committed to one company.

Are you establishing the right interaction with your customers? Do they believe that you care about them? Have you articulated *exactly* what it is that makes you different and why going with you as opposed to someone else matters?

If they don't see the difference then you didn't do your job as a salesperson. If they do, then you will have a customer that will stick with you.

Not too long ago, I got a call from one of the salespeople I mentor. He asked me, "Mark, I want to close this account by Tuesday so that I don't walk into the board meeting without this deal. What should I say to the customer to get them to close by Tuesday." My answer? "Tell the customer you want to close the deal by Tuesday so you don't walk into the board meeting without the deal closed and you want to know if there is any way to make that happen." Complete honesty… what a concept, right? Guess what? He closed the deal. He had to give a little on price, but he got his deal.

Another salesperson asked me, "Mark, a client just told me they wouldn't buy my product because they don't use services like ours in their process. I'm embarrassed that I didn't do better market research to know not everybody does this." My response, "Tell them that you assumed that they would use services like yours because their competition does." Result? The customer became intrigued enough to find out more about why their competition used services like theirs, and ultimately decided that this product needed to be part of their process.

Yet another salesperson asked me, "What do I do when a customer wants to know whom I see as my competition?" I say, "Tell them exactly who you competition is and how they are better and how they are worse."

Total transparency is something that prospects will respect you for. It will also build trust in you and your company.

Once you have that trust, you will find that in general, people like to help people. So, when you call and ask for that deal, and you are honest about why you want to close that deal by a certain time, prospects that trust and respect you will generally do what they can to make that happen. It's not a guarantee for a sale, but it certainly is something that may help you get the deal sooner.

There was an instance when I had developed rapport with a prospect, and the deal was dragging out for a very long time before being closed. I had a trusted relationship with the prospect, and I called one day to find the status of the deal. When the prospect told me that it was going to take another week to get the deal done, without really thinking, I said, "John, I know that closing this deal next week is no different to you, but if I bring this in before the end of the quarter it's about a $5,000 difference in commission to me. Another week delay is just killer to me. Is there ANYTHING we can do on this?" I didn't expect anything, but my relationship with the prospect was so good, that he made it happen. He respected my honesty, my transparency on why I was pushing, and he wanted to help make it happen. In return, I made sure he was a happy customer throughout his experience with that company.

Clearly (pun intended), there are times when you cannot be completely transparent in the sales cycle, but in terms of determining the close, I am a huge proponent of explaining to the prospect exactly what you need/want to get the deal done. They will respect you for it – and may even reward you with the sale for it.

FAIL 7 OUT OF 10 TIMES, YOU MIGHT BECOME A LEGEND

One of the most frustrating parts about being a salesperson is the constant rejection, the constant stream of failure. The more neophyte salespeople I work with, the more I see the frustration over this simple fact of sales. Sales is a numbers game. You can't win them all, and you have to get out there and talk to lots and lots of people to find those people that need your solution, have the means to pay for your solution, and decide that you have the correct solution against all the other alternatives.

Your failures teach you important lessons about how to listen to the rejections and get the yes, and your track record will certainly improve over time. Great salespeople use their sales managers and mentors to refine their pitches, and constantly learn how to get better. But the ugly truth is that you will probably fail more than you will succeed.

As I was watching a baseball game recently, on the big board came a statistic for a player who will be a Hall-of-Famer someday, and very likely a legend in baseball. This man had just slightly less than a 300 batting average. This means that for every ten times he has gotten up to bat, he has failed seven times. For every ten times his fans, his coach, his manager, and his teammates counted on him to perform at bat, he let them down seven times – yet he will become a legend.

Look back through history. Very, very few of the legends we know did much better than this. Ty Cobb's lifetime batting average is 0.366. Only a handful of players ever got over .400 for a single season, and no player has ever finished a season above 50%.

The fact of baseball, is that, just like sales, the system has built into it the knowledge that individual failures are part of the game – and therefore the game and season have built into it the concept of individual failures – and that when you look at the team under the long term lens, that the best still rises to the top. The same is true for companies and their sales organizations.

Thinking about the reasons for individual batting failures:

- Sometimes, the failure is just because the player is off his game. It's certainly very difficult to be at your best all the time when you play many, many games each week. The same is true of sales. Not every salesperson will be able to find the right pitch, the right words, and the right counterargument every time. But in both cases, practice is essential to get better.
- Sometimes, the failure is because the pitcher is just having a great day, and can outsmart the batter – or knows the batters weaknesses and takes advantage of them. In sales, your competition is working the same prospects as you. It's essential to know everything about them, their products, and what their pitch is so that you can be prepared to overcome that.
- Sometimes, the batter is dinged because someone else fails (error). In sales, there are a lot of times where there are very obvious wins that are lost OR cases where you get moved forward in a pipeline discussion because of your competition's misstep. It's important to capitalize on these, but never assume they will happen.

The only way to get a hit is to swing the bat. And, if he finds success three out of ten times, he just may become a baseball legend.

Salespeople need to know that losses happen all the time, and it's a big part of the way sales works. It's hard to know if a prospect is right for your offering unless you find them, talk to them, and try to sell to them. Many of these prospects will be strikeouts, but that's okay. You need to focus on getting as many wins as possible – but know that even the legends fail more than they win – in both sales AND baseball.

Of course, it's the constant stream of failure that makes a win taste that much sweeter. Hold onto that when your sales batting average takes a dip.

SOCIAL TOOLS ARE MAKING SALESPEOPLE LESS SOCIAL

Several years ago, I joined an Internet company as a sales rep, and in about 3 months, I became the top salesperson. At the national sales meeting, one of the other reps came up to me and asked how I was having so much success. I responded, "I'm honestly not that sure that I'm doing anything revolutionary. It just seems that these people are happy to take my call and after explaining the product and how it solves their problems, they are willing to buy." He stared at me blankly for about a minute and then said, "…You call them?"

I'm very much in favor of the trend to social tools. Social tools have given tremendous power to salespeople. LinkedIn, Jigsaw, Twitter, Foursquare, Facebook, etc., are all great ways to research, network and get yourself into a company in ways that were not possible 20 years ago. However, there is this trend in people of a younger generation to rely too heavily on these tools to get the job done. It's true that many younger people will meet their spouses online, will keep in touch with people online, and will continue to interact on-line, but deals get done when people talk to people.

The best salespeople that I have dealt with aren't afraid to pick up the phone and talk to people. They are especially not afraid to get in front of people. When I started in sales, trying to get a sale over email was frowned upon, yet today I meet salespeople who don't leave email/Twitter/Facebook to try and get 90% of the way to a sale. It's this over-reliance on the tools that hold them back.

I see start-up after start-up thinking that the magic of "being viral" and the social glue will propel them in sales. These salespeople and start-up founders think that somehow the magic of the social Internet will make their company profitable. But far fewer companies succeed in this way. Salespeople need to reach out and connect to get the product sold. They cannot be afraid to do so. The more successful the salesperson, the more likely that person is out talking to people.

In order to crush sales, you need to be a social being. And that does NOT mean that you have 600 friends on Facebook, 10,000 followers on twitter, and 800 connections on LinkedIn. It means that you are actually connecting with people one on one. That device in your hand is a phone and it has voice capabilities. So use them. It's very likely that you will see your sales explode.

TUCK IN YOUR SHIRT

At the risk of sounding old, I'm going to spend a little time writing about a trend in sales that has massive implications for salespeople at start-ups.

The entrepreneurial community, particularly in tech entrepreneurship, has a tendency to dress down too far. It boggles my mind when I see decent entrepreneurs who get their big chance to pitch in front of the best VC's, or give a presentation in front of thousands of people- and they are wearing jeans and a T-shirt. It's their chance to make the best impression they can as to why someone should believe in them and why someone might give them millions of dollars.

And, yet, they don't even tuck in that T-shirt! Or they are dressed like a total slob. Hair unkempt, torn jeans, sandals, sweatshirts, or worse. Seriously? Is this "new way of doing business" really professional enough? Am I supposed to believe that you care about your business and your customers when you don't care enough to comb your hair? If you can't put on a pair of pants without holes in them for ME, then how do you present yourself to your customers and prospects?

Am I supposed to believe you are brilliant because you are a slob?

How does this relate to sales? Salespeople who dress and think professionally perform better. This doesn't mean three-piece suit or even a tie. A nice pair of pants or even nice jeans, and a golf shirt (tucked in) at least shows that you care enough to be a professional. Is this "old" thinking? Perhaps. But since I consistently demolish quota, perhaps there is some logic to it?

If you work in a start-up, you need every bit of professionalism that you can grab. Already you are at a disadvantage because people are nervous that you will survive, that your product actually does what it says, etc. Do you need to add another question mark over your head?

Your management should subscribe to this as well. At one firm I worked at, I asked my CEO to come to one of my closing meetings at a very large well known brand, and he showed up hair uncombed, wrinkled shirt (not tucked in), jeans, and flip flops (not even nice sandals). I don't think I need to say that this company was not very successful despite the fact that I had lined up some very high profile deals. Whatever credibility and momentum I had built was quickly erased when my CEO didn't care enough about the prospect to believe that he needed to make himself presentable.

As a salesperson, you ARE the face of the company to your prospects, and when you don't care about your appearance, you set a tone for the company that is something less than professional. It may seem trivial, but it matters. It matters even when small companies sell to small companies. Show me you care about yourself, and I'll translate that to how you probably care about taking care of my account. Show me how you are too important to tuck in your shirt, and I'll know how you will probably treat my account.

Be professional. Dress professional.

BE ON TIME

This really goes without saying, but being late for a meeting or appointment is a very, very quick way to kill a sale. Be at least 15 minutes early if arriving in person (security may hold you up) and there is no harm in waiting in the lobby or the parking lot if you are too early. If you are on a call, dial into the bridge early or make sure you call right at the time you are supposed to call.

If you don't make an appointment in the sales process a priority, then you probably aren't going to make any of my issues a priority after I buy the product.

When you are in the middle of building your startup, you may find that your offering is lacking in many areas. Often, this is simply a result of timing, and it's not what you want to have happen, but just a result of "we haven't gotten to this yet."

Salespeople in a start-up very often want to sell in the best light possible, so they sell to the road map, which is not a bad thing. Being able to use the upcoming features to help the sale along and not give someone a reason to use something else or do nothing is a wise sales choice. When a customer points out a deficiency or hole in the offering, you can simply point to where you plan to be in the product and when.

However, it is highly critical that you never make that roadmap an obstacle to the close. You should be looking for the way the customer gets value today and how you can deliver them that value. If your customer gets too focused on the one thing in the roadmap that they think is important, it is your job as a salesperson to make sure that you help the prospect see how they can still get value today. While they may get increased value down the road, you need to show them that buying what is already released will still provide them value. Your start-up released their product, typically called a minimum viable product, at least, so there should be some value that you can find.

If you see that the customer cannot get ANY value from what you have today, but indeed needs that one item that you will have in the future, table that customer until that feature is released. You aren't doing the customer or your company a favor by closing the deal and promising something that you cannot yet deliver. When those new features are released, you get a chance to go back to all those prospects and look like a hero that listened to exactly what they wanted and delivered.

You should be working closely with your product team on realistic timeframes, but in all honesty, you should be doing anything and everything to make sure you are finding prospects and convincing people about the already released features. Never should you be prospecting on road map features – use them only when you need to move a customer along or convince them that you are on the same page as them — and then get back to showing them why what is already release makes sense to them.

When you sell stuff the company has not yet delivered on, even if you get the sale, you likely won't see commissions until those features are delivered. You will not create friends in the teams that have to design and then deliver the product, and you create tension that doesn't need to be there. If there is no potential customer for what is already delivered, then you are probably at the wrong start-up. More likely, those people exist, but you need to look harder to find them.

The best thing in a start-up is to always focus on selling the stuff you already have and then sell the new features once they are released.

YOUR SALES MANAGER IS A TOOL

There is a big difference between being a salesperson and being a person in sales. What actually makes you a salesperson instead of just a person in sales? You CLOSE deals. And the more consistently you close, the closer you get to being a great sales person instead of just a good salesperson.

A true salesperson does what needs to be done to get the deal done. Sometimes that means sweetening the offer. Sometimes it means dropping the price. Sometimes it means explaining the benefits better, or comparing yourself against the alternatives. But a good salesperson always figures out what's holding up a deal and then looks for ways to overcome that obstacle/objection and get the deal done.

However, very few salespeople can achieve and crush their quotas without the use of tools. The tools in a salesperson's bag include the obvious: the cell phone, the laptop, the iPad, smartphone, the nice suit, business cards, etc. There are also the increasingly important software tools like salesforce.com, Hoovers, Jigsaw, etc. As a sales manager, part of my job is to use these tools to make sure that the sales PEOPLE use these tools to get more sales! To track progress, to uncover deals slipping away, to help lagging salespeople.

One of the more frustrating conversations that I have with salespeople is over important deals (or ANY deal) on the one-yard line that is not closing quickly

– and I'm not part of the process. The BEST salespeople that I have ever worked for come to ME first when a deal is slipping away or stuck or otherwise. **These sales people know that their sales manager is the best and one of the most important tools that they have in their bag of tools.**

Salespeople have egos which are sometimes too big – we can all agree on this – but there is NO shame in getting your sales manager to help out. **THAT IS HIS/HER JOB**! I see too many salespeople try to close the deal 100% themselves because somehow doing that makes them feel better about their progress. I say, doesn't getting the commission check feel better? Too many salespeople try to work around the sales manager and then look like a hero because they brought in the big deal alone.

In reality, who gets the biggest praise from the sales manager? The salesperson that closes the most deals! The salespeople that close the most deals make the best use of EVERY resource placed in front of them. And this includes the sales manager. Salespeople and sales managers are typically aligned in compensation.

As mentioned in how to run proper pipeline calls each week, sales managers will review and try to find these deals that they should be helping with, and force themselves into the deal. Force the salesperson to get them on the phone, or send an email, or call the gatekeeper's boss, or whatever needs to be done. Yet, sales managers hate having to force us into the deal. Salespeople should be reaching out to the manager at every turn to have the manager help close the deals or move them along.

One of the best salespeople I have dealt with is the master of this. She calls and emails me several times a week with tasks for me. She will email me with precise details of whom she wants me to send an email to and, if she hasn't supplied me the exact words, she will give me an overview of what she wants my email to say. I will oblige and help her move the deal along. She will also give me a call list. This list will be VP's or otherwise that she needs me to call as the **grey hair** and move the deal along. She will give me a synopsis of what has been happening on the deal since my last interaction and how she thinks this move will help it. Sometimes she isn't sure how I can help, and we discuss if I can and what the right move is. Sometimes she just calls me and asks me what my opinion is on how to move a deal forward and if she is doing is correctly.

Wow, she uses me, her sales manager, quite a bit. Is she weak? Is she untalented? NO. She is the opposite. She is hands down one of the BEST salespeople I have ever worked with and she makes and breaks her quota consistently.

What has she figured out? She has figured out that her sales manager (and for that matter ALL of her senior management) are tools that she can use at her disposal to close deals.

Once you figure this out – and get over your own ego – you will close more deals.

Use your sales manager. They are one of the best and most underused tools.

Determining the best way to price and deliver your product will likely be your next challenge, and it's not one that will be any easier than any other step.

You will need to provide a lot of freedom and exploration in how best to do this, but finding this is the key to determining the repeatable sale. And the repeatable sale is the key to success.

EXPERIMENT

One of the things that you must constantly do in entrepreneurial sales is experiment.

You need to experiment on price, on pitch, on the offering, and essentially everything about the product. When you experiment, you learn about what the issues are that are the most important and also what the levers are that will draw the actual close out of a person.

Experimentation can lead to learning that your price is too high, or that people want to pay monthly instead of annually. Experimentation can tell you that one particular feature drives sales more than other features and can lead to shifts in marketing or product direction, which can drastically improve the results for the company. Most entrepreneurs today understand that playing with your messaging and keywords in organic and paid search helps you to learn about the product and what will cause an uptick – and therefore it should be an easy extension to apply this to sales techniques.

For example, at one of my start-ups, we played with offering different levels of users, and also different price packs – ultimately learning that our initial assumption that companies wanted to pay "per user" was dead wrong. Our customers were willing to pay MORE for an unlimited pack because it meant they only had to ask for budget once rather than each time they had more users. Lesson learned. Sales prevailed.

Another time, we experimented with messaging. The product spoke to many different aspects of the business. Sometimes we led the conversation with the "functional" aspects of the product – what it could do for them in terms of increasing productivity, and other times we lead with "safety and security". In conversations, we always talked about both, but sometimes we stressed one over the other. This was not always random… but was often thru just a little bit of research about company goals.

One really important way to experiment is with the "non-commit" offer. Offering something that is phrased as a non-committal is a great way to get to the root of an objection and to learn about your product. For example, you might say, "I can't guarantee that my boss will go for this, but if I let you pay monthly, would that change your mind about buying this week?" If they say yes, and your boss doesn't want to make the offer, you have a way to go back and not take the deal. But perhaps after you hear "yes" 10 times, you realize that offering your product with monthly payments is what you should be doing from now on.

What you should NEVER do is lie in your experiments. Blatant outright lies will only come back to haunt you and may actually set you up to fail – both as a salesperson and a company because lies in sales follow you.

For example, NEVER inflate your price and then claim that you are taking percentage off the price to get you to the same or other price. Yes, I am aware that retail outlets do this all the time, and people are used to it. But in anything other than retail, it simply smells rotten and slimy and will get you a reputation.

Never lie about features your product has, or customers you have landed, or your roadmap unless you are prepared to deal with the consequences. I've had bloggers, reporters, and competitors that try to catch me in a lie. And if they ever had, I'm sure they would make sure the world knows it. Ask yourself if the risk you take is worth it. I say that it rarely is.

When you experiment, you need to assume that your prospects will see ALL sides of any messaging/offer/otherwise. If you can easily resolve the discrepancies, then you are okay. Imagine getting the call from the prospect where she says, "I was told by you that your list price is $5,000 and I'm going on the site and seeing that the price is $4,500. Why are you charging me more?" and you are unprepared to let her know why? Then you have a problem. Your answer cannot be that you were experimenting with some new pricing because she will want to know why you didn't offer her the experiment. Most likely you will be caught in a lie and will lose the sale as well as the respect of the prospect.

If you are A/B testing, are you prepared when two people in two different locations bring up your site and see completely different pricing? If you can't resolve the discrepancy, then you will lose the deal. Perhaps change the price on different packages, or different length commitments, or otherwise, but simple differences in prices based on how you surfed the site or what salesperson picked up the phone when you called? Not good.

If it's different messages that you are giving, do they resolve to the same core product? Do you know that ultimately, you aren't saying something that just isn't true just to see what happens? That will certainly backfire on you.

The bottom line is that you should experiment at will, but what you shouldn't do is experiment with untruths or with shady tactics that you can't resolve if you get one prospect seeing both sides of the coin. There are PLENTY of ways to experiment without needing to resort to shady and slimy tactics, so stay away from those.

Honesty is really the best way to go. Always.

EASIER TO BUY = EASIER TO SELL

One morning I went to buy a cup of coffee. This coffee shop charged $1.95 for a cup of coffee – after tax it was $2.11 per cup. I watched as the line grew and grew while the cashiers made change for each person that tried to buy a simple cup of coffee. I even saw people walking away because the line was getting too long. I wondered why this shop didn't change the price just to make the act of buying a cup of coffee that much easier. There is a LOT of margin in a $2 cup of coffee – and by simply lowing the price (even a penny) they could have made buying the coffee that much easier and I would argue, made more money in the long run.

One of my clients was suffering a very similar problem. The way they were selling the product was not aligned with how the companies could buy the software. They attempted to charge a "per-use" or rather a "per-user" fee, when in fact, the only money the departments had to spend was capital improvement budgets – meaning pay once a year and that's it. So, we tried a new pricing scheme which was a single price per year for all-you-can-eat. It was wildly successful.

Sales isn't easy. When you make it hard to buy, you make it that much harder to sell. The coffee shop needed to have pennies available, needed to make change, and ultimately made the buying experience an awful one for the sake of a few pennies. Had they changed the price of the coffee so that I paid $2 including tax, then I would have been in and out of that shop in a few seconds and they would have been onto the next person in line. No one would have needed to worry about coins. I'm actually wondering whether I will even go back to this shop based on my experience. Is that what was intended? I think not.

For complex projects, it's even more important. Today, we have so many ways to make the sales process easier; we need to take advantage of this to make our lives easier as salespeople.

As an entrepreneur, you need to understand how your customers buy, and how they can more easily consume what you sell. If you make this process transparent and easy, and then give them a simple way to buy, you will see sales increase. Remember when Radio Shack used to ask for 15 pieces of information such as phone number just to buy batteries? Well, I went to Radio Shack this weekend, and simply swiped a card and walked back out. They've finally figured out that easier to buy = easier to sell.

If you are having trouble getting people to buy, have you thought about:

- If the WAY you charge is just too difficult to buy?
- Do your companies allocate budget in the way you ask for money?
- Do you only accept credit cards, but the company can only provide PO's – or the other way around?
- Is subscription billing a difficult way for your customers to buy – and they would prefer once a year?

- Or perhaps once a year means they need a capital budget – but subscription fees are low enough that your decision makers have automatic signing authority?

You need to probe and get the answers to these questions because the easier your product is to buy, the easier it will be to sell. The easier it is to sell, the more successful your company will be.

STRATEGY MUST INCLUDE AN UPSELL

Upselling, despite what some people believe, is not a sneaky or dishonest sales strategy. In fact, it is an essential strategy for start-ups. I do, however, understand how many people can see it this way.

At the bagel store near my house, a bagel costs $0.49. Yet, order that bagel with $0.03 worth of butter, and the bagel is suddenly $1.69. Why does the store do this? Because it's great to advertise bagels that cost only $0.49, but who comes into the store and only orders 1 bagel with nothing on it? The upsell is the critical method of driving profit into the store.

It's not a dishonest strategy, but if you sat there and really thought about what is going on, it's kind of maddening. And if you listen to the entire process of people walking in and out of the store (which, as a person who looks for sales techniques in anything, I do), you will hear the constant upsell. "Can I interest you in a coffee too? Perhaps some cheese with that pork roll sandwich? Can I interest you in home fries?" The entire sales process is hinged on the upsell.

Think about every infomercial you have ever seen... "But, wait… act now and get a second for only $19.95 plus shipping and handling."

I can see how people think of the upsell as a technique that lies on the border of sleazy in terms of sales tactics.

However, it is an honest and essential tool for start-ups that sell to enterprises. As I wrote above, one of the major keys to seeing breakthrough sales processes in start-ups is to make the decision to buy an easier one.

For most start-ups, especially for those in technology, buying from you takes a major leap of faith. They have to trust that:

- You will survive until next year.
- That all of your claims of success to date are repeatable. After all, you are basing your past successes (assuming you have some so far) on a very small and statistically insignificant base.
- Your product even does what you say.
- That you have the ability to scale.
- That you won't embarrass them to their boss, their investors, Wall Street, their customers, etc.
- That you won't disappear with their money.
- That your visionary new way of doing something will even work.
- And dozens of other ideas around working with an unknown entity.

All of their fears will surround ideas like these. Therefore, the larger the leap that they have to make, the harder it will be for you to get the deal done.

How do you solve this problem? The intentional and explicit upsell. You need to create a snack-size version of your product, and get these people committed. Once you get them hooked, if your product is as good as you say and provides them value, then they will happily upgrade to the larger package. Buying anything from you is a massive leap, so you need to figure out the best ways to make the leap smaller. You should avoid the free trial if at all possible because you want to establish the relationship of customer-vendor as quickly as possible rather than customer-prospect. It's too easy for a prospect to say yes to a free trial, when they really have no intention of buying.

Lots of companies have embraced the upsell with the freemium models that are so common now in cloud-based products, and that's a great thing! In fact, it's the entire beauty behind the cloud model. By allowing someone to buy in smaller chunks, and with an upgrade/upsell path to a larger commitment, you make getting on board significantly easier.

The tricky part here is to make sure that you provide enough value in the lowest version, and enough differentiation and value to get people to move up to the more expensive options. I can't generically speak to what must be included in the minimal package since all products are different, but it should be enough to have the company understand the value that they will get. It also needs to make them feel comfortable with your company enough to write a large check. There are entire discussions about what and how you should position your packages. Assuming you've embraced my logic behind the upsell, you need to really think about how it affects the sales process, particularly in how your prospects buy. Do you really understand how the buying happens in their company? Do you know what the threshold is where the decision maker can buy without major approvals? Do you know what the budget process is? Do you know what the fiscal year is? Do you know how add-ons (upsells) are treated? You may offer something at $2,000 per month with an opportunity to cancel at any time, but the person buying your service may need to budget for the full $24,000 just in case they use it for the full year. Once again, you need to realize the size of the leap that the prospect needs to make in order to buy. Is your minimum level, when multiplied out for a year, still too much pain for the prospect? And, while you think you are only asking them for $2,000, they are making a $24,000 decision, which is a very different decision. Can they make a $24,000 decision without needing to bring the decision to a C level person OR can they make a $10,000 decision on their own? If so, perhaps your initial offering is $10,000 with an upsell from there.

There is no generic correct answer because every product/offering/value prop/prospect mix is different, but I strongly believe that the start-ups that spend the time to figure out the correct upsell strategy will have better results with selling to larger enterprises.

WOULD YOU BUY YOUR OWN PRODUCT THAT WAY?

Everyone buys things and everyone has opinions on where they like to buy, how they like to buy, and what makes them buy. Why then do so many companies forget these experiences when they plan out their own sales strategy and pricing models?

When talking with entrepreneurs and their sales teams, an exercise that I like to go through is to have them think critically about their own product and its sales cycle. Then, I like to have them really think about how they buy similar products and what the experience has been for them. The results of the exercise are very often quite interesting and reveal why some fledgling products have trouble getting traction in sales. A great deal of it boils down to a particular view of what and how you should charge. It also uncovers that some feel "justified" in charging something or using a particular sales tactic. You need to know how you would respond to situations if you were on the other side of the table.

Some examples:

The over-aggressive sales guy: I had a conversation with an entrepreneur recently that was directing his salesperson to call and email, call and email, and call and email these prospects until he got an answer from them. One customer said, "Call back on Monday." Sure enough, on Monday at 9:30AM, he was questioning why the call hadn't been made. Later that same day, he complained that a sales rep had been hounding him to make a decision, and he was frustrated that this sales rep had no appreciation for the fact that buying his product wasn't the most important thing on his list. Hmm... seems like a pretty evident disconnect. This entrepreneur's revenue pressure was causing him to force the exact aggressive behavior that was irritating him by another company because he was under the pressure. Taking a small step backwards and looking at the situation critically, he should have recognized that aggressive sales tactics often don't work. He was fully aware of that fact, but forgot it.

Set-up Fees: Another company recognized that in order to get their product up and running for a customer, they had a significant effort that they had to deploy, and therefore they decided that they needed to charge a setup fee in order to re-coop that cost. Yet this same management team resisted a setup fee for a service they were deploying because it made the initial pain very difficult, causing that decision to take about 6 weeks longer than if no setup fee were charged. Do I think that looking at their setup fee in a vacuum that they are justified for wanting to charge a setup fee? Yes. But I don't know anybody that likes paying setup fees. It also makes the decision for the prospect needlessly harder. When you are trying to make the most sales you can in the shortest amount of time, adding obstacles to the sale will only hurt you. If you charge $5,000 per month, and your setup fee causes a minimum 6-week delay in the sale (if you get it at all), then your setup fee better make up for the $7,500 you lost by even **HAVING** a setup fee. When this customer was challenged on it, the response was still that it was labor intensive to set up and therefore a setup fee must be charged, when in reality the setup fee was just an obstacle. Think about it from the customer's perspective. If paying a setup fee is painful, then don't do it! (Or understand that sales may suffer)

Free Shipping/Promotion Codes: How many times have you left one site for another site because one site charged for shipping and the other one didn't? Have you not bought on a site because they didn't offer (or your couldn't find) a promotional code? I've worked with entrepreneurs who forget this simple lesson. Don't you like to get a deal? If you see a promotional code field, but have no promotions, do you frustrate your sales targets? I worked with a client who justified that he needed a shipping fee, "because the shipping costs really hurt my bottom line." Is this true? Probably. But his target market was accustomed to no shipping fees. Therefore, even though he was justified, he was using a practice out of the norm that was hurting him in terms of sales. Once he looked at it from his customer's perspective, suddenly he figured out a way to overcome the shipping dilemma (offering free shipping over a particular cart amount).

"In your face" selling: Most entrepreneurs I talk to, during the exercise, talk about how they hate when a site/email/ad has so many calls to action that it feels slimy. But when I look at their site/emails/ads, it looks like a late night infomercial with "BUY NOW" messages plastered all over it - or very transparent language that attempts to lead you to a purchase. I'm certainly not a conversion expert, nor am I a design expert, but I know slimy sales when I see it. Take a critical look at the marketing materials you have, and ask yourself if you'd be offended by what you send – or question its tactics.

Difficult return, cancellation, or trials: The most important thing to me when I sign-up for a new service is knowing how and when I can cancel, provided I don't like the service. Once I do this, how do I delete my data? How can I make sure you won't pester me or use my information? These are the things I think about when I sign up for a service and I know many people who agree with me. Yet, I have clients who create their service and purposely make it difficult to cancel. Why? The reasoning is that if it's easy to cancel, people will cancel. If your service is good, people won't cancel. Knowing, and trusting, that I can get out of our relationship is a faster path to get INTO the relationship. Ask yourself about how you would feel if any of the subscription services that you use made you feel like you were being held captive?

All of us buy things. We buy small things and large things. We know what we like in that process and what we hate. We cannot forget those lessons when we decide how we plan to promote our product.

For many companies, this is a critical problem in their sales DNA. It's very easy to think about how you'd *like* to sell your product and how you'd *like* to get paid for your product. But it's not about you; it's about your prospects. And, if you were your prospect, would YOU buy from you? Would you like the way you were being treated? Would you trust the person on the other end? If you can't unequivocally say yes, then you need to re-think your sales strategy/tactic/pricing.

DON'T BE AFRAID OF ENTERPRISE PRICING

I've certainly given you an argument for making your product low priced in the beginning and implementing an upsell, but I want to explore the counter argument as well – enterprise pricing.

When I was selling software in my first start-up, the world of software was very different from what it was today. Other than small consulting projects around my software, I never sold anything for less than $200,000. The idea was to have few clients each year at a high dollar amount. I sold a large enterprise-wide solution to Fortune 500 companies. This included desktop software, server software, database set-ups, and more. Each of my software sales had an 18% annual maintenance that included product updates, phone support, and more.

I will admit, when the whole cloud revolution started, I was quite resistant to the change, and certainly did not see the immediate path to success in cloud mode. This feeling was for several reasons:

- Having years of product development on a desktop application, I wasn't exactly hot about starting over our development onto a web-based solution.

- Advanced web technologies were not yet available and my competition's products that were evolving were insipid in comparison.

- My clients and prospects were not yet warm to the idea of having their data external to the enterprise. They still wanted to have all the data within their own data centers. (A factor that has changed considerably; most companies are comfortable with this now)

- And most importantly: it was hard to leave that enterprise sale! Getting a big six or SEVEN figure check from a client to go to a model where you get a LOT less was something I was having a hard time wrapping my brain around.

Nonetheless, I knew this was the inevitable direction of all software, so I worked hard to figure out how to get our product on the cloud.

What we did was take our desktop application and remove the "client-server" communication guts. We replaced it with web services, and ultimately were selling a desktop application that communicated across the Internet and data was stored in the cloud. We sold it for $35 per user per month – which was actually an acceptable price to our new prospective client base. (Market research showed that $100 per month was the threshold and our software plus a mobile device lease plus wireless service totaled about $100). The new prospect list was not only the Fortune 500 companies, but also every small business that had field service reps: every landscaping business, every delivery business – essentially anything with a dispatch function.

We were mildly successful with this approach and would have been more successful with it as time went on. However, the market crash of 2000 was tough on this business and we wound-up retreating. As many companies today are aware, in order to build a cloud business, you need a lot of customers. That means that you have to do a lot of marketing and a lot of sales. It takes a while for the recurring revenue to get to a level that supports your business, so you need funding in order to bridge that initial gap. What I did was to fall back into enterprise sales. I could fund my company for many months if I could close a $500,000 sale – and I could weather out the storm.

While I had the opposite question, the question that many cloud-based start-ups need to ask themselves today is: Should I start slow and get lots of customers at a small price or is there a way to bring enterprise sales and pricing into the mix? Getting big checks to run your company holds off investors, creditors, and gives you breathing room that you control. Is there a way for you to package up your offerings, or increase them, and as a large bundle sell a large ticket item to a Fortune 500 company? For many companies there probably are, but just as I had trouble thinking initially about the web 2.0 sale, I'm sure many start-ups will have trouble figuring out the enterprise sale. –But I'll bet it's there.

Here is an example: I have a start-up client that makes software that is typically charged on a per-use basis. Corporations sign-up for an account, but they are not charged unless they use the service. In my sales plan design session with this client, we talked about how to turn this into an enterprise sale. How? By going to a corporation and offering them an unlimited-use package for up to 30 users, in exchange for a twelve month paid contract. It has been mildly successful, and although it's not the ultimate direction the company is going to take, it is bringing cash into the company in a much quicker way, at least for the short term.

While organizations (and individuals alike) love getting cheap and/or free services and software, larger corporations that are going to consider using a start-up service, will feel better knowing that you have some cash to survive through their contract. Therefore, your enterprise sales pitch should show how you have thought through how you are going to service them for the long haul and that the enterprise sale is the way to that end. You may be surprised at how some companies will embrace paying you a large check because they will have MORE confidence in your survival than if you take nothing and they rely on your service, they are certainly invested in your survival.

Customers that pay you more will expect more from you because they are paying more, but you will probably get richer adoption from the customers that elect this method. Of course, you need to make sure that your plans don't get 100% hijacked by these clients, but it is certainly worth looking at how to add this type of sale to the mix, even if it's just a bundle of services paid up-front. It's a tough but rewarding sale.

DOC...ITS MARTY...YOU GOTTA GET ME BACK TO 1985

1985 was a great year for me.

- I started high school.
- I met my wife (although we started dating 11 years later).
- I was tapped by the Superintendent of Schools to design and build a computer system to run the schools grades, scheduling, rank, attendance, etc.
- I started my first real entrepreneurial endeavor of some random computer consulting, training, and repair for some side dollars.
- I became one of the lead drummers in the school drum-core.

But, all of that considered, unlike Marty McFly, I never want to go back to 1985. Why? In terms of sales, the 21st century provides so many great and inexpensive ways to sell better than you could in 1985.

Once, I went looking for some software on sales compensation planning and I found a company that was offering a free year license of their software. I was intrigued enough to ask for an account. I entered all of my information, and in a short amount of time, I received an email giving me instructions on how to get my free account. I was given the option to watch a series of about 18 short videos OR I could attend a webinar on how to use the software. Since I wanted to get going right away, I opted for watching the videos.

I painfully watched all of the videos. It was good that they broke them up into 18 separate videos because, if it were not for my needing to click on the next one, I would have drifted into a complete coma. The videos were decently produced, but without being able to click in the software, none of what they were showing me meant anything to me. It became hard to follow.

After I finished watching all the videos, I looked to see if I had access. I did not. 24 hours later, I got an email from a salesperson telling me that since I hadn't supplied a phone number, that I couldn't get set-up. I replied that I didn't need to talk to anyone that I just needed access. I then got a reply that he would see about getting me setup as soon as possible because they could see that I had viewed all the videos, even though this was not their normal policy since they had not spoken to me on the phone. Some 24 hours later, I got an email with some login information. I had trouble logging in because it was not 100% obvious to me that they had changed the user id and password that they asked me to supply. Despite the fact that they had asked me for my email address and password during set-up, they set me up as user1@mydomain.com and some generated password. As I was figuring all of this out, there were several rude exchanges between the salesman and myself. It was obvious that I was circumventing his ability to upsell me, even though I still hadn't even decided if I wanted the base offering. Once I did get logged in, I was thoroughly disappointed in how difficult the software was to use and navigate. It became clear why they wanted your phone number and required viewing to the videos; the product interface was horrendous and difficult to use.

What amazed me throughout the process was how 1985 all of the sales tactics felt. This is era of web 2.0 and of freemium. This company was using a requirement of a phone number so that they could talk to me and attempt to upsell me additional services (which is how this company makes money). They use their webinars to rope in additional customers and sell additional services. There is nothing wrong with the upsell (I'm a fan) and with the model of wanting to talk to the prospect. But the sales technique needs to work the way business is done today. There was no reason why I couldn't have been given access to the software and THEN spoke to a sales rep. Or, that I could have been given the option to pay for one month and then perhaps gotten an upsell call after that. (I would have gladly paid for 1 month).

I will compare this experience to one that I had with a CRM I was investigating. To sign up for this product, I clicked on "sign-up now." It did not even require any payment info. I got a full account and after I logged in, I saw several places where I could click on videos to explain each feature if I was confused. They also had a very well stocked knowledge base and blog for additional information. I was able to look and find most of the information that I needed to access. And, when I was lost, I got feedback and email replies quickly from their staff. I was never asked to talk to someone, and they never tried to upsell me in the initial phases of using the product.

I am now paying this company every month for their software. Why? Because the sales process was clean, genuine, and I was able to see and play with the service before I spoke to a salesperson about additional services. The salesperson was accessible – but not in my face – and I was able to move forward at my own pace.

In 1985, without the ability to provide software as a service, and without the ubiquity of the Internet, much of this was not possible. But, we have to realize that it is the 21st century now and we need to sell according to our environment.

Some lessons learned here:

- **Let people try your solution.** There is no reason NOT to when it's software as a service (SaaS). It's easy to turn them off if it doesn't work out. It's not 1985 where you are shipping out a disk, working through an install, etc. Let them in and let them explore and play on their own. By providing access to a community, videos, blog, etc., you can let your customers help each other and get a much more rewarding and valuable experience.
- **Forget the pre-upsell.** I don't know anyone that likes to be upsold when they haven't even seen or used to product yet. You will have plenty of time to do the upsell later on. Let people become members of your community before you start attacking them for more money. In 1985, you didn't get easy access to your customers to make the upsell. Today, your customers come to your site every time they use your software and you have plenty of time to do the upsell. And the upsell is much more valuable when they are already tied to your solution.
- **Let the customer do some of the work.** Why did this company ask me for login information and then just manually create new login information completely unrelated to what I provided? There was no reason for them not to let me provision myself and actually create a

username and password that works for me. In 1985, I may have needed to do this for someone, but today, you can let your customer fill in some of this information for you. After all, they know it better than anyone.

The ultimate lesson here is that you can't get caught in old ways of selling. The Internet and cloud computing provide some very exciting new ways to sell and deliver solutions. In fact, there are new and exciting ways to sell everything. Our customers have come to expect this model of sales and it's actually very aggravating when you encounter a company that doesn't subscribe to this new model. We are working on Internet time now. Compare my two experiences: one set me up in minutes and got my business. The other took days and by the time I got into the software, I was so soured by the experience, unless the software was amazing, I wasn't going to be hooked anyway.

So, as great as 1985 was, I don't ever want to go back. Sales in the 21st century is way better.

LONG SALES CYCLES ARE NOT OK

Once, I sent a note to an entrepreneur friend of mine whose company was doing well, but I heard through the grapevine that he needed some help in the sales department, things just weren't moving along as fast as he would like them to. So I reached out and let him know that I had some cycles available if he wanted some help putting together a sales plan, and figuring out how to accelerate his growth.

He very quickly and politely replied that the type of sales planning and assistance that I do at QuotaCrush really wasn't applicable because, "his product has long sales cycles and long lasting relationships."

I sat there confused and bewildered for a few moments and then realized that perhaps he was missing something very completely obvious. If your sales cycles are long, perhaps that is a result of the fact that your salespeople don't know how to shorten it. One of the biggest differentiators between good salespeople and great salespeople are those that know how to close and especially those who know how to close quickly. Sometimes, this means

133

getting the customer "half-pregnant" or hooked on your product in a small way will create a small close, and then follow it up with a larger sale as previously discussed.

To be satisfied with a long sales cycle means to be satisfied with mediocrity. I challenge anyone with a long sales cycle to find the shorter sale. It exists. It always does. Part of what I show companies is how to find that smaller and quicker sale. When you resign yourself to a long sales cycle, you will try to find salespeople who can tolerate a long sales cycle. Who are salespeople who can tolerate a long sales cycle? "Good" sales people; not great ones. By definition, they are less hungry and less cash focused, which is what you want them to be. The one exception to long sales cycles is companies that sell exclusively to government agencies who are usually tied to large budget cycles. EVERY other corporation has ways to spend money now to solve a critical problem. Not every corporation will buy the shorter sale, but there will be some that will buy the shorter sale, shrinking your overall sales cycle. Unless you think like this, you are doomed to accept the long sales cycle, get your investors to accept the longer sales cycle, and end up in a spiral downward.

What should you do? Challenge the long sales cycle at every turn. Challenge your sales team to shorten in. Challenge your product team to build in ways that help the sales team get people a taste that wants them coming back for more. This is the path to real success and building a sales engine that produces consistent and predictable results.

The second part of his sentence was also troubling to me. He didn't want someone short term because he needed long-term and long-lasting relationships. A top mistake that companies believe is that people keep buying from you because there is a relationship with you. In the martini lunch, this may have partially been the case, but it is no more. Companies will buy from you consistently because you solve their problems. I like to think I'm a great relationship guy and I've done sales for lots of companies. What is great is that those customers STAY customers after I leave. They aren't tied to me. Why? Because I sell value and I sell great products that solve problems. It's not about me. I get that. It's about the problems that the product solves. If that product solves the problem that the company says it will, then those customers will outlive the product. A salesperson's relationship might be able to smooth over problems with the product based on relationship, but that isn't why my friend needs long-term salespeople. And if you are planning for problems, then there are bigger issues at play. You should never be worried about how long your salespeople will be around in your hiring process if you believe that you have a great product that solves a big need.

I responded to my friend with a note summarizing this concept, and I have heard only silence since then. My guess is that he truly believes that he has a unique situation and long sales cycles just need to be accepted. Great salespeople know this is never the case, but I suppose that is why so many companies struggle with sales. There are established beliefs that are hard to escape.

The reality is if sales aren't where you want them to be, if you aren't closing fast enough, you need to question if you have the right team, the right process, the right pricing, etc. Challenge it all and accept nothing as a fact of your sales cycle.

WHY BUY THE COW?

As I mentioned in the upsell lesson above, you should certainly be providing a small sampling of your product, be it crippled or otherwise; however, when dealing with large enterprises, you will quickly find yourself in a situation where you are being asked to give more and more without a commitment. It is very important that you resist urges to do this and get the companies to make a commitment.

Here is the basic issue with dealing with large organizations: You are an entrepreneur. This means that you have ambition. You are a salesperson. You understand risk and you are able to go and ask for what you want. You are not intimidated to move things forward. If you are, you won't be in business long. For the most part, your prospects in large corporations are NOT these types of people. They live within the bureaucracy of a large corporation and are often crippled by it.

What this means is that while they love your offering, they may not be able to pay for it. They may not even have the authority to bring it into the organization, and the organization may not be willing to even look at what you do for a wide variety of reasons.

Individuals within large corporations will take what you give them and wave lots of carrots in front of you. "You know, GlobalMassiveCorp could buy a lot of your product, you should be offering this for free to me. If I were someone in your shoes, I would." But, the sad reality is that more often than not, the individual you are dealing with is not empowered to make a strategic corporate-wide decision for GlobalMassiveCorp if they are even empowered to make it for their department.

Yet, that person will try their best to get you to give them more and more for free.

I say no. Give them a taste like you did in the upsell plan, and no more.

Immediately, I will get push-back on this because, well, we do need to get them in the door, and we do need to make concessions for bigger organizations AND the bureaucracy that they have. Indeed you do, but you also need to flush out that this has any chance of being a real deal: the right decision makers, that there is budget, that this person has the authority, and that they aren't just fishing around.

So what is the best way to do this? With the "out clause."

Provide a contract or otherwise which provides all the terms of the deal, and give them x days to back out of the deal with NO cost to them and no questions asked.

When I used this tactic at my first start-up, it would look something like this:

I would set an installation, a set of acceptance criteria, and a series of installments or objectives that varied on the type of installation, etc. The company would have 60 days to evaluate the software and accept or reject the software. I would then also provide a sliding scale:

- If rejection was made in 0 to 60 days after installation, 100% of the first installment was refundable.

- If rejection was made in 61-90 days after installation, 75% of the first installment was refundable.
- If rejection was made 91-120 days after installation, 50% of the first installment was refundable.
- If rejection was made 121+ days after installation, 0% of the first installment was refundable.

The idea here was to force the prospect to start the process – all the hard stuff – the legal, the pricing, IT, whatever would be involved once the sale was made – but at the same time I made it zero risk.

If the person on the other end didn't have budget, or was afraid to bring it to legal, this would bring it to the forefront right away. It often became very clear that there was NO way they were going to bring you to legal OR that it was going to be a six month process. But it was better to learn all of this up front. By presenting the solution this way, I was able to get to the bottom of the real sales process much more quickly and start the negotiations.

HOW TO SELL COW POOP

A few weekends ago, I saw a truck come and deliver cow manure to two of my neighbors. It got me thinking about packaging and how really, anything can be sold, when it is packaged correctly.

Think about cow poop. I have no idea how large this market is, but I have to imagine it is pretty darn big. And people sign up year after year to willingly let someone deliver a truckload of cow poop, dump it in a big pile on their driveway, and then they take this stuff in wheelbarrow loads and spread it all over their yard.

In sales, it's important to understand that the right message, the right pitch, and the right packaging of the product can make the difference between phenomenal success and failure. If someone said, "Hey, want to buy some of my cow poop and spread it on your lawn?" it would probably not sell as well, yet packaged as "fertilizer" it is suddenly a HUGE market.

This is NOT about selling someone something they don't want or need. In fact, the cow poop on your yard is EXCELLENT in terms of what it delivers as nutrients for the plants, the lawn, the flower garden, etc. Buying and using cow poop is a GOOD thing. Nobody is getting swindled here; however, in order to get the product out, you need to make sure that the packaging of the message is done correctly.

When I approach selling, I try to always look for the pain of that particular customer and craft a message and story around that pain. This is not disingenuous. In every company I have worked for, I honestly believe in the product I am selling and believe that it will be a good thing for the prospect. The key is to craft the right message that makes sense to them, that identifies why the product will solve THEIR problem. Whenever I have lost faith in the product's ability to do that – or in the direction of the company – then I know it's time to move on. I find that unless you believe it, it's hard deep down to sell it. At least it is for me because I honestly want to bring the RIGHT solutions to my customers

The anatomy of a sale includes finding people to pitch to, getting them to accept the pitch, and then getting them to buy. While it's true that it's that last part that separates good salespeople from great, most sales are lost in the pitching phase. If you don't make a compelling reason to continue thinking about your product, I can guarantee that it won't go any further.

While much of what constitutes a good pitch for a start-up is not different from established companies, as I've said before, everything is heightened and under intense scrutiny. If "nobody ever got fired for buying from IBM," then I would say that lots of people probably got fired for hiring someone other than IBM, especially if they took a big risk on a start-up. Since this is the case, your job during the pitching phase is critical, and you must work very hard to make your skills here are of the highest quality.

In this section, some common sense and some advanced sales pitching techniques will be explored.

NOBODY CARES ABOUT YOUR PRODUCT

The first important, yet difficult, lesson that any salesperson in a start-up needs to learn is that nobody really cares about the product you sell.

Prospects care about their own problems, their own issues and their own pain. They don't care about your offering.

The only reason they are interested in your product at all is because it solves a particular problem of **theirs**, makes their job easier, saves them money, keeps their boss off their back, or some other selfish reason. You can think your product is as cool as hell, but people don't buy something cool as hell, unless they understand how it helps them. Yes, your prospect will be thinking about his/her own issues while you talk about your product. If he/she can't make a match, he/she will not buy, no matter how cool or sexy your product is.

Think about the purchases you make in your life. Rarely do people make purchases simply on the features that they see. While it's true that many people make impulse purchases based on features, but it's rarely based on those features alone. I don't fish, so I have no need for a fishing pole, or fish-finder, so no amount of features is going to get me to shell out any money for the latest fishing gear. However, I will gladly drool over the latest portable electronics devices. Why will I drool over one and not the other? It satisfies a need in me; something that I want to make better in my life. I'm on the road all the time, and having portable electronics that satisfy my entertainment, connectivity, information, and other needs is critical to my everyday pain. Now, if a fish-finder salesperson could somehow show me that the fish-finder helps me make more sales or find information on my prospects, then I may suddenly be interested.

Once a salesperson understand this fact, the sales process changes to what it needs to be – about your prospects' problems, issues, and pain. The faster the salesperson gets to relating the product or solution, and more importantly the features of the product or solution, to the *particular* pain of the prospect, the faster they will get to a sale.

Time and time again in demos and presentations, I see a salesperson super intent on getting all of their points out. They are so intent that they do anything and everything to make sure that they cover all the slides they prepared and that they demo every aspect of their product – even when the prospect has told them what they need and what they care about. It makes me cringe when I see a salesperson get to a section of their presentation and the prospect says, "That's interesting, but here is my problem… and I want to hear about this…" and then the salesperson continues on their defined tour of all of the product features. As a salesperson, you should first focus on the features that will help solve the prospects greatest pain.

If you can't define that, then you haven't done your homework, or there is no match for your product, and you will never get the sale. If you only need a single feature to sell the product, why not focus heavily on that feature until is exhausted and the prospect fully understands it?

Once you get your prospect over the hurdle of understanding how you solve their problem, then you can start to talk about all the other features and things that will make it even better, perhaps taking their business in a new direction.

Salespeople should be the greatest evangelists for their products and they should know and love the product. By knowing the product that well, the salesperson should be able to talk to anyone and quickly ascertain what part of the product, if any, can solve this prospect's pain, and get the prospect to understand that too. If you, as a salesperson, feel the need to just vomit all of the possible features onto the prospect hoping something sticks, you are expecting your prospects to do your job and I certainly would not expect you to crush your quota.

Your prospects will never care about your product until you MAKE them care about it. How? By showing them how it makes their lives better/easier/simpler/richer. Focus on them instead of your offering and you will sell more.

SALES SELF-SABOTAGE

There are hundreds of ways to kill a deal with words you use in a presentation. The worst way of all is self-sabotage, yet it happens all the time with start-up salespeople.

Self-sabotage is the use of particular phrases or language that essentially kill your deal for reasons that have nothing to do with the offering, but with the way you treated your customer. In cases of self-sabotage, it's typically a very innocuous or accidental statement, or a misinterpreted statement that causes the pain and kills the deal.

Self-sabotage comes in many flavors (and by no means is this list exhaustive):

THE UN-INTENDED INSULT

When you build your start-up solution, it is very often to solve a particular problem, or a recognized weakness in the current way of doing things. Therefore, the unintended insult is very easy to do in a start-up.

The salesperson says during his pitch, "We developed this solution to make your employees more productive." Or "our product stops companies from wasting thousands of dollars."

In both those cases, you are telling the prospect that they are not being smart about their current operations. While possibly true, the fact is that without your solution, they probably were doing the best that they could, so they weren't wasting money or being less productive. They were doing the best they could with the tools available. You are going to make it better.

But, you just told them that they are wasteful with money and resources. That is an insult. You didn't mean it that way, but it can come across that way.

LET ME EXPLAIN FURTHER, DUMMY

There will be a lot of times that your customer won't understand what you are showing them, even in a normal discussion. Sometimes, they may ask the same question twice.

Never, use any sort of wording like, "I'm sorry, let me explain this again." Or "I think you didn't understand what I said or meant, let me show you again."

What you are doing here is essentially telling your customer that they are too dumb to understand, so you'll be happy to explain it again.

Instead, just answer the question again happily, or explain the concept again without bringing notice to the fact that you had to do it twice. Maybe they weren't listening, or daydreamed, or maybe they ARE dumb – just don't call them out on it.

THE ACCIDENTAL REVEAL

There isn't a company or a product in the world that hasn't had problems, but you definitely do not want to let prospects know too early. You might say something like; "This feature is really great, especially when our servers go down." Wha-what!? You have outages? If this wasn't the part of the discussion where you talk about your amazing reliability, you just revealed something you weren't framing in the right context.

Every industry has its set of buzzwords, acronyms, short hand, and other inside language. You should never assume that your audience knows any of this. They may or they may not. Assuming it is clear self-sabotage.

Especially in the start-up world, new start-ups and technologies are created all the time. As someone in the start-up community, it's easy to get caught up in the latest trend, the latest technology, etc., and then immediately assume the rest of the world knows it. "You don't use <insert 6 minute old start-up here>!? Wow! It's great, you really should!" This makes me feel old and out of the loop. Perhaps, "I found this new tool called <insert same name> and I've found it to be quite useful." Subtle difference, but the second is considerably less threatening that they have not been in the loop on the latest stuff.

Sales self-sabotage is essentially having completely unintended consequences to things that you say, whether in your pitch or in other conversations. You need to be very mindful of what you say and how you say it in your sales pitches so that you can avoid this very common issue.

SALES LESSONS FROM A 2 YEAR OLD

Think about a typical conversation with a two year old:

Tina: "Daddy, can I have some candy?"
Daddy: "Not now."
Tina: "Daddy, can I have a cookie?"
Daddy: "It's two hours until dinner, not now."
Tina: "PLEASE!"
Daddy: "I said no!"
Tina: "Can I have an apple?"
Daddy: "Oh, alright. Fine - have an apple."

While some may read this conversation and determine that I am a pushover, I want you to read into the persistence of the two year old. Not once did Tina think that she wouldn't eventually get something to eat, she just needed to figure out the right words and the right win-win solution so that she could get what she wanted. And she did!

She didn't give up once she heard the first "no." She thought about it, and changed her pitch until she ultimately got what she wanted. Now, perhaps it wasn't 100% what she wanted in the beginning, but in the end, she got a snack.

Is my daughter a born salesperson? Perhaps, but this is the nature of every two year old. Somewhere along the way, many of us forget this lesson of persistence.

In your own pitches, you shouldn't be taking no for an answer. That doesn't mean you should hound your prospects like a two year old, but you should make sure that you are getting the no, because there is absolutely no way to get a yes. In the conversation above, my daughter wanted a snack, but figured out that I wasn't against a snack per se. I was against junk food. By determining what I was okay with, she was able to get what she wanted. She found the win-win.

Ask the right questions, think about the problem from their side, and understand that a "no" isn't always a "no" – it's just "no - in the way you've presented it"

GETTING PAST A GATEKEEPER

When trying to call into a company and get to the decision maker, often you can get a direct dial. Other times, you have to go through an assistant or operator in order to get to speak to the decision maker. The gatekeeper's job is to make sure that only important conversations happen with the decision maker and keep out the riffraff. With that knowledge in mind, you need to figure out ways to not become the riffraff.

I gave a speech in NY a few years ago and got into a very lively discussion on the best tactics for getting around a gatekeeper. The following list is a compilation of the ideas that we talked about. It is a great starting point for ideas on getting through.

1. **Give the gatekeeper the benefit of the doubt.** Most salespeople assume that an assistant doesn't have the time, judgment, or influence to help them, and therefore ask immediately for the decision-maker. Huge mistake! Treat every assistant with the courtesy and respect of a CEO. Doors will magically open for you.

2. **Treat the assistant like a human being.** This is obvious, but most assistants don't aspire to be assistants forever. Google their name. See if they blog or tweet. What's their web presence? Find something that they are genuinely interested in and run with it.

3. **Use your arsenal.** Make a joke. Play good cop/bad cop. Talk about the weather. Mention a tidbit you saw in the news. Ask about their company's latest release. Ask if they're running the company yet. Whatever your style, get the assistant on your side. After all, they're controlling your access to the company. There's no need to make them enemy #1.

4. **Write down the assistant's name.** Refer to them by name, every time. Be friendly, polite, and direct. Remember that you are not yet their highest priority, and being impatient, self-righteous, or vague is never going to get you there.

5. **Be honest and forthright about your solution.** Value the assistant's time - it's just as important as the decision maker's. Explain to them up front what you are calling about and why you think it will add value. Don't hang up and try again if your target is unavailable – it's disruptive and dismissive. Worse, you've wasted an opportunity.

6. **Ask for help.** The more you can engage the gatekeeper in the process, the better. Ask the assistant about the best time to call, the easiest way to get in touch, direct numbers, cell phone numbers, etc. Ask if it's better to leave a voicemail, leave a message, or just to call back. But before you do that...

7. **Assume the assistant is a decision maker.** Believe it or not, the assistant's job isn't to keep you at bay. Rather, their job is to discern potential value for their executive and/or their company. By that logic, you should involve the assistant's judgment as much as possible. Gatekeepers have an ear to the ground about every aspect of the business. Ask them about their pain points. Where would they

see the most value added? What's most important this quarter? Next quarter? Next year? What's their growth strategy and what are their bottlenecks? What's their biggest frustration? Assistants offer unique insights that can help you refine your pitch.

8. **Ask who else is involved.** Gatekeepers have the ear of everyone that will be involved in your sale. They know whom you should be talking to. Ask if you are targeting the right person. Do they know anyone that might be of assistance? Who should you talk to first and why? Who is the ultimate decision maker? Let the assistant paint the relationship structure for you and guide you up the ladder.

9. **Alleviate their burden.** Assistants are responsible for sourcing and evaluating vendors. If you've called them at the right time, you've eliminated their legwork. Let them be responsible for walking your sale through the company. Don't blow it by presuming that they won't be involved in the process.

10. **Let the gatekeeper advocate.** If you've effectively engaged the gatekeeper, he/she will be your advocate throughout the entire sales cycle. Let him/her make introductions on your behalf. Ask about the best ways to engage various decision makers. Ask his/her opinion on what's most important to each decision maker. Use him/her as a strategic sounding board as your deal goes through the pipe. The more he/she is engaged in the value, the more value he/she adds to you.

All of these ideas boil down to one basic theme: be nice. If you are nice to assistants and gatekeepers, you have a better chance of getting to the right people.

THE SALES ONE-LINER

As a sales manager and mentor, I've had to critique a lot of sales people on their style and offer suggestions about how to do it better. And, in giving the pitches myself, allow those salespeople to critique my own sales style and determine whether they buy into my style or not. All of this is done, of course, to figure out ways to close more deals and crush quota.

One of the tactics that I nearly always use, which has been pointed out by nearly every salesperson I have worked with over the past several months, is the "one-liner." At some point in the discussion about the product or sale, I will make one small slightly humorous line to lighten the mood – or otherwise get the prospect smiling. I honestly didn't give this tactic much thought before it was pointed out so many times, but after analyzing it, I understand why I do it.

The sales process, for both sides, is usually a rather stressful exchange with people continually trying to figure out the other person's thoughts and determine how to get what they want (and make sure they don't get ripped off). So, by lightening the mood, or trying to ease tensions, you can help the process along. After all, if you're reading this book, you are the type of salesperson that isn't about figuring out how to manipulate your prospect. You are about trying to find the right solution at the right price for them anyway. Making sure that tensions stay low and assure them that you are trying to find the best win-win solution is the one of the best ways to make the sale.

Sample One-liners from one month:

- While attempting to finally close the deal with a prospect and feeling that there was still doubt on her side, I said, "Mary, our product will make you so much money, you will buy gifts for my children." She responded with a big laugh and "Oh my God you are a salesman – but I like your confidence." Deal Closed.
- After about 10 minutes of the prospect essentially giving quite explicit reasons why he thought that our product wouldn't work for him, I allowed about 30 seconds of silence and then said, "I'm not 100% sure, but something tells me your aren't a believer." After a big chuckle, he said, "Yeah, I'm certainly not sold and I was being pretty clear about that. But tell you what, if you can get me information on 1, 2, and 3, I'll take a closer look."
- One of my salespeople called a prospect that said, "Oh God I thought you were one of my ex-wives calling looking for my money." She quickly responded, "Oh I'm calling for your money, I'm just not an ex-wife."

What most salespeople should take away from this is that lightening the mood and easing tensions in the sales process is critical. In terms of delivering witty one-liners, you should really think about whether this exact tactic would work for you as a salesperson. Not everyone's personality will conform to this type of strategy. If you aren't someone that speaks like this in normal conversations, then it is perhaps not something that you should try in your sales career. I don't consider myself a comedic genius, but certainly my personality has always been one that incorporates humor into everyday situations.

In terms of how a salesperson should deploy mood lightening in their sales career, it's very individualistic. If you go with this exact tactic, then you should make sure that you can think up, and deliver properly lines that will actually move the process along and not interrupt the process. If the above examples were not delivered in a witty way, it could certainly disrupt and even kill a sale.

NEVER VOMIT ON YOUR PROSPECTS

While it may seem obvious that you should never vomit on your prospects, it's a very common move that sales people make.

I'm not referring to actually spewing your chewed lunch onto your customer – but spewing WAY too much information.

The easiest thing to do at a sales-call is to just talk and talk and talk. This rarely leads to a sale. When you are more focused on getting all of your points out, and less on what the customer wants to hear, you are essentially losing lots of opportunities to learn and respond to what the customer needs.

One of my least favorite phrases that a salesperson says is, "That's a great question and I'm going to answer that later in my presentation." This is the sign of a salesperson more concerned about getting all 27 points out rather than identifying the needs of THIS customer. Sales meetings should be ways of identifying how and whether you can solve a problem the prospect has. Your product may have hundreds of great things in it – but there may be one small feature that solves such a large pain that it's enough to make the sale and the rest is gravy. You need to root out and identify that pain, focus on that feature and identify how to solve that problem. When the customer asks

148

something, rather than tell them you will discuss it later, take that opportunity to learn why they are asking that question and find the problem they are trying to figure out if you solve.

Yes, this will derail your presentation, but you must know your product well enough to allow the customer to take you in any direction they want. After all, the meeting is about THEM not you. Take every opportunity to listen to them and close your mouth. Avoid vomiting.

Another time when salespeople word vomit is answering a question. For example, "Does your product work internationally?" Wow! For a vomit lover, this is a great chance to spew out 10 minutes on how great the product is internationally. What's the right answer? "Why, is that important to you?" And then sit and learn some more.

SWINGERS MAKE BAD SALESPEOPLE

We are in an age where sharing information about oneself is very common. In many instances this is a very good thing, as it is in finding information on your prospects, and figuring out how best to sell to them. In other instances, it can work against you.

As a salesperson, you are on display all the time, and you never want to frustrate or anger your clients, especially on topics unrelated to the sales process. Would you sit in a room with a prospect, not knowing their political views and start ranting about a particular issue? Or worse, would you use foul language and slurs against people in the political landscape? If you are a smart salesperson, of course you wouldn't.

Yet, I see intelligent business people who have public twitter profiles, post regularly on blogs and more spouting off the same type of stuff – in that type of tone. As a salesperson, you need to understand that in today's world, everything you post, tweet, send or otherwise place on the Internet is fair game in your sales career. Have an opinion and feel free to even comment on it in a constructive way. But be careful how you start wording things and making fun of things, and monitor the language you use. It can make you seem juvenile and undisciplined. And worse, it can anger and upset your prospects. You need to use discretion in what you spout out.

This also extends to Instagram/Facebook or any other place where your information is displayed. No prospect wants to look you up on the Internet and hear about your conquests, or drinking binges, or worse. It can kill your sales prospects, and you may not even know why!

One time, I was sitting down with a customer and we were signing the contract for a very large deal. The company was located in the Bible belt and the managers that I was dealing with were very conservative and obviously strong in their particular convictions. He told me why he chose me over my competition in what was a very tough sales process. He decided to do an Internet search on my competitor and my company, including the salespeople with whom he was dealing. He found a page where the salesperson of my competitor and his wife were advertising themselves as swingers. He didn't feel comfortable doing business with someone like that, and the deal was mine. To be honest, for what the customer needed, my competitions product was better, yet I still got the deal because my competitor didn't use discretion.

This is no particular judgment on what anyone does in their private life, their particular political views, their family structure, or otherwise. In fact, that is exactly the point: None of that matters in most situations. There are exceptions to this if you are selling something that is particularly slanted towards one view, but for most products and solutions, a personal opinion has no place in the sales process. Therefore, keep it out of the sales process. In order to keep it out of the sales process, keep it off the Internet.

Are you losing deals because you are sending out flames about the presidential candidate you hate? Are customers chuckling about you behind your back because of pictures of you at that weekend party while they sign with your competition? Do you not get a callback from a prospect because a Google search turns up unflattering information?

Just like you should not word vomit on your customers, you should not vomit about your life and your opinions. Every comment you make, everything you post, is part of your sales career. Make sure you remember that as you click "submit."

In sales there is a rule that many sales people know, and that is, "he who talks least wins." And of course, there is the old adage that God gave you two ears and one mouth and you should be using them in that proportion.

When you give a sales presentation, you should remember that it is a presentation – a chance to **PRESENT** your solution/product/offering. When you **PRESENT** something, you are offering an *introduction* to it so you should be providing your overview, and then be using the rest of the time to determine how, if at all, you can solve your prospect's problems.

A lecture, on the other hand, is a LONG period of time, with one person talking. You know, that hour or two hours that you were forced to sit through in college, forcing yourself to stay awake and taking copious notes. Considering that it is hard to remember what was said, it's hard to stay awake, and you just wish for the end, why would anyone think that turning a sales presentation into a lecture is a good thing?

Yet, too often, I see salespeople use their pulpit as a chance to lecture about their industry, their vision, their insights, their successes, etc. But the truth is, no prospect really cares about all of that. As I said, they don't even really care about your product. They care about their problems and how you can or cannot solve them. It is true that you should be looking for ways to connect with your prospect, but a lecture is not a good way to accomplish this. It may be nice to be able to pontificate and show people how smart you really are, but the thing that will make the sale is not your IQ. It's that you are smart enough to solve their problems. The only way to know what their problems are, and how you can solve them, is to LISTEN more than you talk.

The worst part is that if you ask a salesperson who talks too much about how they felt a sales meeting went, they will likely feel better about the meeting the more they spoke and showed how smart they are – rather than thinking the meeting went poorly because they didn't listen to what the customer wanted. Again, the truth is that they are not going to sign on the dotted line because they are bowled over by your brilliance.

You need to judge a meeting by how much information you **OBTAINED** not by how much information you **CONVEYED**. Only once you have all the information, can you best win the sale.

THANK YOU SIR, MAY I HAVE ANOTHER

In sales, there will be times when you will get a flood of rejections. As you get rejection after rejection, you have to stand up, and try to get the next sale, no matter how much losing that last sale hurt.

But isn't the whole point of becoming great to get fewer rejections? Indeed it is, but the facts remain that no matter how good your sales process is, there are customers that just cannot get the budget for your product, regardless of how much more efficient it will make them, how much money it will save them, or how much it will increase their own sales.

Think about your own life. In my own house, it would probably make a lot of sense for me to replace the windows. The old ones are much less efficient than new ones would be and I'm pretty sure that most of the gas between the panes is gone. I probably would get an ROI on the window investment in about four years. I plan to be in my house for more than four years, so rationally; this is a purchase I should make, right? Well, like most of you, I have many things I'd like to spend money on or save for, and I need to determine what and where my cash is going – often not in a rational way.

Your prospects are going through this same type of struggle as they decide whether or not they should purchase your product. This means you need to have a bigger pipeline, patience with clients, and more creativity in how to price and sell your product.

So as your pipeline paddles you over and over again, it's important not to lose momentum and not get discouraged. Find the reason that you are doing this and focus on it.

In order to avoid growing discouraged by all the rejection, you need to find your rock, and focus on it. When that happens, you will find it much easier to deal with the rejection – and also keep you focused on your end goal.

FOCUS ON WHAT NOT THE HOW

When I started as a sales rep at one company, being a salesperson with a fairly technical background, I immediately asked for a login into the software so I could start playing around and learning the software. My boss informed me that I would not receive, nor would I *ever* receive a login into our software.

His reasoning? If I started to go into the software, I would focus on HOW the software could do certain things and IF the software could do certain things in a certain way, rather than focusing my sales activities on finding the right customers and identifying their pain.

Granted, I had a sales engineer who would make sure that the things I was selling were actually possible in the software, but this tactic of my manager's was a major stroke of genius. In the 18 months that I was there, I was very focused on making sure I could find value for the customers. I had enough of an understanding of what was possible in the software to make a lot of sales, but what I didn't get concerned about was whether the way they wanted to do it was difficult or time-consuming. I only worried about selling on the basis of the value it brought the customer.

When a salesperson gets too deep into the workings of the software, they put an imagined obstacle in front of themselves when they know that something the customer wants to do is not easy to do in the software, or doesn't work 100% the way the customer is accustomed to. When I didn't have a detailed understanding of how the software did certain things, I was forced to keep my sales conversations around *what* the software did for the customer in terms of their business improvement and marketing goals, rather than focusing on *how* the software would accomplish their goals in detail. The sales engineer handled those details. By that point, I usually convinced the customer so much on the VALUE of the software, that the WAY it worked didn't matter, even if it wasn't exactly the way they would have wanted it to work.

It very easy for a salesperson to fall back on a demo, or discuss features, rather than to stay focused on the software big picture – which is the REAL reason that anyone will buy it.

Regardless of what type of solution or product you sell, it's important to keep focused on what it is you are giving the prospect and then help them see the how.

When you pitch your product, you should be focusing on the value that you provide and if YOU understand the value ABOVE the noise of how the software does it, you will actually be better at finding the proper solution for the customer.

If you can sell the customer on WHY the software makes sense for them, and you've spent the time to understand HOW the software does that, then you can develop an internal champion. If the customer is "closed" in terms of value, then actually completing the close becomes much easier. They become your internal sales tool, because THEY will look for ways to overcome the objections.

Here is what I mean:

Sales Scenario 1: You go on your sales call to showcase the software, discuss how it can improve processes, and how it's so easy to configure, etc. You get to a screen that is more complicated than the prospect is used to seeing. In fact, all the configuration possibilities scare the prospect. The options are there because you are selling a generic product and you think it's great and you are proud of the configurability. Yet, it scares the prospect because you're potentially adding complexity they don't have or don't understand. Now, you try to explain why it makes sense overall. As you plead your case, in the back of the prospect's mind, he is thinking about the software and how it may cause him pain to get running.

Sales Scenario 2: You go on your sales call and talk about the value of the software. You discuss what it has done for their industry, how it saves money, how it improves processes, testimonials, etc. You take the time to understand their process as it stands today. You build a trust that you KNOW the industry and that *you* understand the pain that *they* understand. Then, you start crafting a better process in their mind, which ultimately maps to your software, but you aren't showing your software. Perhaps you show a small screenshot here and there, – but you never log into the software.

If you've done your job right in Scenario 2, the customer is sold before you get to log into the software. You will know this is the case when they start figuring out the configuration and workarounds of the software once they see it. Why is he willing to live with workarounds? Well, he bought into the VALUE. They know that software can change. If he is a good customer, you will often change it for them.

My proudest sale is one where I convinced a very large recognizable brand to use my software for their core business. They were going to put software from the company that I started in front of their entire ability to generate revenue. I'm proud of it because the first time they saw the software was when I was in final contract negotiations. I sent my VP of Product Development to the tech team while I went to the CIO's office to close the deal. They NEVER saw the software short of screenshots.

They bought on VALUE.

COLORBLIND PROSPECTS

I met my brother at the gym recently, early in the morning. After our workout, my brother asked me to help him pick out the right tie for him to wear to work (He had brought four to the gym with him). Why? My brother is colorblind. Not black and white only, but enough that getting himself dressed can present challenges.

I had forgotten this fact about my brother. I shared a VERY small bedroom with my brother for about 14 years before I left for college. Helping my brother with his clothing choices used to be a regular occurrence, but having not lived with him for so long, I forgot about it. Having him ask me about it reminded me of life in his eyes.

As I left the gym, I related the story in my mind to sales. (My wife will tell you that I relate **EVERYTHING** in my life to sales). The question I asked myself was, "Am I too wrapped up in the way that I see life and the deals that I'm working on that perhaps I'm not looking at the deals in the way that my prospects see them. Do I really understand and know the way that they see the world so that I can better create a win-win scenario that will lead to a close?

155

The good news was that for most deals, I believe that I have taken the customer's point of view into consideration and framed them correctly. A few other deals, I rethought them and am trying some new strategies to awaken them. But, the simple tie question really points out that every prospect and every person within that prospect will see the world in a different way. The way that they see the world will color (pun intended) their view of the world. Unless you, as a salesperson, understand that and build your deal around it, it will be difficult to get your deals done.

Imagine someone trying to sell my brother another tie. They could show him a green tie and a blue tie, and those ties might look identical to my brother. OR, one with a beautiful hue may actually look hideous to my brother. I guarantee that he won't know if it matches anything else he owns so he may not make the purchase regardless. This is a man that thinks denim blue jeans look purple, and thinks Christmas trees have a reddish hue. A salesperson that understood that my brother was colorblind might do a better job about describing the color, matching it to his current suit, or rely on other tools in selling items that are color dependent to color-blind people. Whatever the tactic, if the salesperson never takes the time to understand my brother's colorblindness, he will never make the sale.

Ask yourself; do you REALLY know your clients' challenges? The way they see the world? Do you understand how the economy has affected their business? Is buying your product something that is a great risk for them personally? Do they even think about how to solve problems in the same way that you do? If you are a technology guru, using technology to solve problems is natural. Perhaps your prospect doesn't immediately run to technology to solve a problem. If you are under 30, you may immediately understand the value of social networking, but your 60+ prospect thinks that social networking is a big time-waster.

Whatever the challenge, you need to understand how they see the world, so that you can frame your sale properly. Go back to the social networking sale: Perhaps you need to spend more time discussing why social networking has transformed business. Get them on board with that before you start touting your product where, for another prospect, you can launch right into the benefits of your specific solution.

There are no hard rules here – but just the simple idea that you should always be looking for ways to see the world thru your prospects eyes. And if they are colorblind, simply ignore the fact that they may be wearing a mismatched tie.

SALES LESSONS FROM THE GRAND BAZAAR

One of the nicest things about being in sales is getting to travel to interesting places that you probably wouldn't go to normally. In my career, I've seen nearly the entire US and several countries. A couple of years ago, I got the opportunity to travel to Istanbul and it was an amazing experience. I am very intrigued by historic sites, particularly the events that shaped the world we live in today. But actually planning a trip to Turkey wasn't high on my list. My family would much rather travel to more relaxed vacation sites that require less thinking. As a salesperson that travels, we are often at the mercy of where our families want to go when we do get fun travel.

I was fascinated by Istanbul: the history, the beauty, and the culture. One of the many sites that I visited was the famous **Grand Bazaar**. The Grand Bazaar is a massive market with over 1,000 shops selling everything including jewelry, clothing, food, trinkets, and more. The trip through the Bazaar gave me a fantastic chance to view lots of different sales styles, tactics, mistakes, and successes.

The overarching style of sale in the Grand Bazaar is one of haggling. There is no set price for anything. The vendors and the customers all understand that haggling is the mode of operation here. I set about a number of purchases to investigate the sales style of some of the vendors.

UNDERSTAND YOUR PROSPECTS' ALTERNATIVES AND WILLINGNESS TO WALK

My first purchase was a toy gun for my son. To me, a beautiful replica of an Ottoman Empire Blunderbuss with a mother of pearl inlay seemed like a great purchase for a boy of seven. I asked the vendor how much the gun was. He said it was 90 lire. I said that I only wanted to pay at max 50 lire. He then showed me some cheap guns at about 30 lire. I said thanks and started to walk away. He grabbed me back and said that he could do 85 lire for the original gun. I said,

157

"Sorry but I only want to pay 50 lire for something for my son. If you can't do 50, then I'll find something else." He went to 75. I said, "50." He said, "I keep changing my price, but you stay the same." So I said, "Okay, 51 lire." He laughed, put the gun in a bag and said, "60 lire." I handed him 60 lire and went on.

I respected his tenacity and salesmanship, but he saw that I didn't have that much attachment to the item, and was willing to walk. My willingness to walk was not a tactic I just wasn't that attached to the item. But at 60 lire, approximately $40, it seemed like a decent deal. The challenge that this vendor, and all vendors there have is that there are 50 vendors selling very similar stuff in a very close proximity. So his challenge was to make the deal as quickly and fairly as possible. By making exchanges short and quickly understanding my pain points and willingness to pay, he was able to quickly negotiate a deal – and get me off my initial price.

When you are selling, you need to understand your prospects ability to walk, their absolute need for your product, their willingness to take alternatives – even if they aren't perfect matches. When you are selling your product, do you know the alternatives that they are looking at? Do you understand why they might choose an alternative? This vendor might have understood my hesitancy with getting a gun home on a plane or my willingness to just get anything for my son.

Once you truly understand why someone will NOT buy your product, you are more likely to understand why they WILL.

UNDERSTANDING WHAT YOUR CUSTOMER IS LOOKING FOR – IF ANYTHING

After I purchased the gift for my son, I started browsing around again, and was stopped by three different people asking me to "check out their uncle's shop right around the corner." These wandering "lead generation tools" are seeking out people on the street to pull them to their shops. When the first person grabbed me, he asked what I was looking for and I told him that I was shopping for my wife. He then took me around to his "uncle's store" and when I got in the store, I was brought a delicious glass of hot tea. I was then shown, in a private space, a series of very beautiful and amazing silk carpets. I acknowledged that the carpets were indeed well made and beautiful (which they were; probably the most beautiful carpets I've ever seen or touched) and kept looking for my exit. After I was shown about 25 carpets, the salesman finally told me that the rug I liked the best was only $10,000 – which he said was a great deal. This probably was a good deal given that it was a very large hand-woven silk carpet with a very complex design.

I explained to him that while I thought the carpets were beautiful, I was not in the market for a carpet; especially not a carpet that cost $10,000 that I would have to cart around the rest of the day and then 5,000 miles back home. He then tried desperately to show me $5,000 and $3,000 carpets but I finally got my exit chance. I thanked him for the tea and went on my way.

I was approached by the "lead-gen" guys to go to their "Uncle's Store" two more times. Apparently, the thing in Istanbul is to have your nephew pimp your store in the Bazaar.

As I strolled through the rest of the Grand Bazaar, I wondered how often this tactic was successful. Were there many people who, when just walking through a bazaar, suddenly decide to drop $10,000 when they went to the bazaar to window shop? If I'm going to spend $10,000, there has been a great deal of consideration on my end beforehand. I was certainly not dressed in such a way that would have given him the impression that I was much wealthier than I am where dropping $10,000 would have been an afterthought. (Or does he think all Americans are that wealthy?)

This salesperson didn't once try to understand me, my shopping habits, my ability to spend $10,000 on a moment's notice, or any of the skills that I would expect someone to have if they are in a high priced product sale.

When you sell your product, do you think about whom you are calling on and their ability to pay for your product? If you are cold calling, do you know if they need or have ever thought about a product like yours? The answer is probably that they haven't, and you need to take this into account. You need to take the time to understand the customer better. This salesperson sat me down and gave me tea, which would have been the perfect opportunity to quiz me on my current buying habits; what do I do for a living? Do I live in a house or an apartment? Do I have a co-financial decision maker (wife) at home who would change my purchase habits on large items? He didn't ask me any of those questions and therefore just threw anything and everything at me in the hopes that something would stick.

It was a very curious exchange and one that I'd love to see stats on how often this approach works.

SPEAKING THE SAME LANGUAGE

My third exchange was purchasing food. This exchange didn't actually happen inside the bazaar, but near it. As I tried to order food and wine, the waiter just looked very confused; they obviously did not understanding anything we were saying. The result was losing precious time. In the end, we had to resort to pointing at menus and pictures before we got our order.

This was certainly not the waiter's fault. I was the one in a foreign country and should have been able to communicate. But it helped to illustrate something to me; Are you and your prospect speaking the same "language?" Are you talking in your native tongue, using buzzwords and phrases that make perfect sense to you, but baffles the prospect?

Too often I see salespeople who are so close to their product that they don't realize that everyone outside of their company has NO idea what they are talking about. You should always make sure that you are speaking in the native tongue of your prospect if you want an easier sale.

I have to say, my trip to Istanbul was educational, successful, and informative. As usual, I found great sales lessons in the trip.

FORGET CELEBRITY

People are people. Forget that they are the CEO, the CMO, the CTO, the COO, or the VP of whatever. Forget that they are phenomenally successful. They are people. They need solutions and appreciate a good solution when one is presented to them, especially if it saves them money, time, or gives them a competitive advantage.

Too often, it seems scary to call into a very important person, or someone you think is intimidating. The worst thing that can happen to you is to get shot down. You don't have the sale anyway, so there is little to no downside.

IMAGINED OBJECTIONS

Any great salesperson will research their clients prior to making the sales call. They will also murder board their pitch, and make sure that they are prepared in every way for any sales pitch they give.

As you do this research, you will prepare yourself for any objections that may come your way. You should not, however, let that research create imagined objections for you.

For example, when I was a very green salesperson, I went on a competitor's web site and saw that they had listed a prospect of mine as one of their customers. I was crushed. I assumed that my competitor had beaten me to the punch and now I was dead in the water. I called the client and questioned him on it. He had no idea what I was talking about. After further research, I found that this prospect had done business with my competitor a year ago and it had not gone well. What was an imagined objection or obstacle was actually something that helped me.

In another instance, I assumed that because I had closed a major name in one industry that other major names in that industry would not be interested, and I shied away from talking about this customer in the meetings. In one meeting, they asked me point blank, and I was honest. They immediately replied that knowing their competitor trusted a start-up was actually a buy sign for them too. I thought the right move was still to shy away from bringing this information up. The point of this chapter is to discuss imagined obstacles I had created in my mind,.

You must always focus on the solution you provide. Understand that often the obstacle that you think is there does not exist. The customer will create enough obstacles and objections for you; don't create your own. As salespeople, we can't let what we THINK are the obstacles get in our way. We need to move forward. If you honestly know that your product will help your customer, then you need to find a way to show that customer exactly how the product solves their problems.

ALL MY COMPETITORS STINK

Every year, when the political battles heat up, I am reminded about a classic sales mistake: bashing the competition.

In politics, I amazed at how many people feel the need to dirty campaigns, and lie about the competition in order to build their own case. Anyone can decide that a certain candidate is not the right choice for him or her. I challenge anyone to find a candidate who doesn't genuinely believe they are trying to do the right thing for the people they plan to serve. There are many men and women in office whose methods of leading I find atrocious and whose views I think are bad, but I never question their determination to better our world. Likewise, most companies out there are trying to solve problems for customers. They may be doing it in a different way than you, but most honestly believe in their method and how it will help its customers.

Recognizing your customers' strengths is essential to creating a successful, customized pitch that resonates well with your customer. You need to recognize that your customer often has a difficult choice about which product to select. If you can, help them craft a convincing argument explaining why your product better serve them. Also, work together to build the argument that demonstrates why the competitor's product is not a great fit. Do this and you will increase your chances of getting the sale.

For example, if I were trying to sell you apples and someone else was trying to sell you oranges, I could bash my competition by telling you that my apples are sweet and his oranges are citrus, and citrus causes acid in your stomach.

162

Or, the better pitch might be to say, "While oranges are indeed a great fruit and have amazing benefits like Vitamin C, I know that someone who is as on-the-go as you are. Both of you will appreciate the tremendous benefits that a fruit like an apple can provide. Apples provide portability (no need to peel it), cleanliness (no juice running down your arm), and are the perfect balance of deliciousness and nutrition. Your prospect knows that you, as well as your competitor, have pluses and minuses. When you point out your competition's benefits, it adds significant credibility to your entire pitch. Your prospect is going to go through this exercise of weighing the pros and cons after you leave. So do the prospect, yourself, and your company a favor by taking the time to go through the pros and cons with your prospect. Not only are you helping the prospect, but you should also take this opportunity to plant exactly what you want them to remember about you and your competitor.

Perhaps the candidates could try to do more of the same.

FEAR IS A FOUR LETTER WORD

Someone asked me recently what I thought was the biggest impediment to sales.

I thought for quite some time on this. Was it bad presentations? Selling to the wrong people? Not asking for the sale? Or even something out of the sales persons control like price or packaging or branding…

After much thought, I decided on one common theme that can kill a sale and a salesperson:

FEAR

Fear can cause the most damage in the sales cycle.

- **Prospecting**: You can't be afraid to call anyone and everyone to get you the meeting. Once I was trying to get a meeting at a major beverage company. I called 20 VP's and spoke to 20 assistants before I decided to call the CMO (Chief Marketing Officer). His assistant got me someone that granted me a meeting. (The switchboard operator and I actually became very friendly!) I wound up doing

163

millions of dollars in business with them. Imagine if I had been too scared to actually call into the CMO office or if I had been too afraid to call the second, third, and fourth people after I had already left messages with others in the office.

- **Presenting**: Once you arrive at the meeting, you need to exude confidence. If you are afraid during your presentation, it will not instill confidence in the product. You have to believe that you can change the prospect's world, save them money, or improve their life. You also need to have confidence to make them understand that. Fear in a sales presentation will be very obvious to all attendees and you are highly unlikely to get the sale.

- **Closing**: You can't be afraid to ask for the sale. Ask for the order and don't let the prospect drag you along on free trials or continual meetings. If they can't make a decision, move on. Very often it's their fear of asking for the necessary funding or of upsetting you. Fear is why you aren't closing it. Force the issue.

- **Negotiating**: This one pretty much goes without saying; your commission most likely depends on getting the most money you can for the deal. Don't be afraid to say no to a price break or a giveaway. But ask for something in return, such as a longer contract term. Negotiating and fear are polar opposites.

- **Post Sale**: Your customer may come back to you wanting more – or trying to change the rules of the deal in order to get out of paying, etc. You can't be afraid to stand up to your customer. And on the flipside, if your company is changing the rules or not honoring the agreement, you can't be afraid to stick up FOR your customer.

Fear and sales do not mix. If you are overcome with fear, you will not be a successful salesperson. Do what you need to do and don't be afraid.

HMM...WHY DO YOU ASK?

Great salespeople love to talk. But, salespeople need to make sure that whenever they answer questions during a sales pitch, they need to understand *why* the question was asked.

The natural tendency when someone asks you a question is to give an immediate answer to that question. However, unless you understand the motivation behind the question, chances are you will answer the question with irrelevant information or with information that will not move the deal closer to the sale. You will have lost a perfect opportunity to learn more about the customer.

I am NOT proposing that you provide untruths or NOT answer their questions. You need to answer the question properly. You also need to make sure you understand the motivation behind the question before you attempt to answer it. This is critical in understanding how you can make the sale. Every question that is asked of you is an opportunity for you to get the information you need to make the close.

For example, you are asked, "Does your cloud-based system allow me to backup my data manually to my own servers?" The inclination will be to instantly provide an answer with the Yes or No and then describe how it works or how you overcome this. For this example, it doesn't matter whether the answer is a yes or no. The customer has given you a perfect opportunity to learn more. The next words out of your mouth should be, "Why is that important to you?" The reasons could be several. And each has its own lesson on how you can get the sale:

- *The CIO won't allow any system in without this feature.* You've learn that you need to sell the CIO to get the close

- *Cloud-based systems with remote back-up have to go through the IT budget instead of mine because I have to have IT sign off on it.* You've learned how products get paid for, and how to design your proposal so that the sale can go thru easier.

- *They had a major data-loss last year.* The shareholders are very sensitive and they need extra re-assurances before they will sign onto a cloud-based service.

- *My company has major requirements for reporting and wants to do it off back-ups of data.* You learn of an opportunity to upsell them reporting services or data transfer services. In this case, a question about backup was actually a question about data export – which you learned by not immediately answering the question and diving in, but by listening.

Outside of these examples, there may be hundreds of reasons why they are asking about remote backup. Some of them would have been helped by a YES answer and some would have been helped by a NO answer. But you couldn't know which unless you asked the follow-up question. When you answer too quickly without understanding the motivation behind the question, it's impossible to know if you have answered it in a way that will move you closer to or further from the close.

Take the opportunity to understand WHY they asked the question and help build an answer to the question that will solve their problem.

Never answer any question until you understand why it is asked.

NO DEMOS!!

Whenever I suggest that a start-up salesperson do no demos, I immediately had about 10 hands go up to challenge my claim.

"But, my company sells video conferencing, and I have to show them how my quality is better than my competition."

"But, unless I show them my great interface, they won't understand how I'm better than competitor X."

I challenge all of this. If you can't articulate the *value* that you provide over your competition, or the value you bring in general without a demo, you aren't going to get the sale anyway. If you make video conferencing software, then tell me that your algorithm was developed through listening to the mating calls of owls or whatever makes your technology great. If I can grasp and believe WHY you built your product the way you did and am sold on your thinking, the demo is icing. If I don't believe it, then the demo is wasted time.

Demos are a chance to screw up. What if the product doesn't work during the demo? You lose all credibility with the prospect and you killed the sale. Convince the customer of the value that you bring to them, and you don't need a demo. If you convinced them of the product benefit, the demo either confirms or kills the sale you already won.

Why are salespeople so shocked by this statement? Because giving the demo is easy. It takes up a lot of time in the presentation. Demos give you the illusion of feeling busy, as if you did a lot to move the sale forward. But, in actuality, you didn't. Spend that same time focusing on how to convince the customer of your value and save the demo for after you've sold them on the value of your product. When you focus on the features of your product, you take focus away from the value that you bring to them.

A few years back, I sold a $2M contract before the customer ever saw the software. I convinced the largest marketer in the world to trust me for text message voting on a live TV program without ever seeing the software. What did I talk about in my sales presentations? The reasons my company was great; how we differed from the competition; how we were providing great service for their competition and other companies in industry; how our algorithms would protect them, etc. THESE are the things that matter, not what my interface looked like. The interface can change, but the reason we were a great company? That is far more difficult to change.

CHRISTMAS TIES ARE BAD SALES TOOLS

One morning near the end of the year, I had a sales meeting. Before I went in, I sent out a tweet that said "business casual sales meetings mean I get to wear my really cool Christmas ties almost never... I think I'm going to wear them anyway..."

I enter the meeting, and the very first thing the man says to me is, "Interesting tie choice. I'm curious as to why you would wear that. I think perhaps you didn't think about whether wearing a Christmas tie would bother me." I was caught quite off-guard and for a moment thought perhaps he was following me on twitter and was making a joke about my morning comment. But he definitely wasn't. He was truly upset at my tie choice.

He had a traditionally non-Christian sounding last name, but I honestly did not think that anyone, regardless of what they celebrate or don't celebrate in December, would be offended or upset at a Christmas Mickey Mouse tie. Little Mickey Mouses in Santa hats were sprinkled throughout the tie. It was perhaps the most secular Christmas tie that existed. I expressed to this gentleman that I honestly thought it would show my fun side and my holiday spirit, but did not think for a second that it would offend or upset anyone. We moved on from the tie discussion, although he brought it up at least four more times during our meeting, making "just like your tie choice" comments.

I have written about how you shouldn't make all of your public ranting and opinions part of the public domain because it all becomes fair game in the sales cycle. Well, in a way, I did that with the tie choice. I screamed to the potential client that I celebrated Christmas and was proud of it.

This example clearly points out someone at the extreme, and not the normal mainstream reaction to a Christmas tie. Nonetheless, it was a reminder that you need to do your homework, and you need to make sure that you understand your audience. I took my eye off the ball, and got smacked for it.

When we express our personal views, they become part of the sales process, for better or for worse. As small as a comment, tweet, blog post, Facebook status update, online photo, email, or other action may seem - it can affect a sale. My tie choice affected this sale. As small as that might seem, it became a factor.

I can guarantee you that my Christmas ties will stay in the closet during sales calls from now on!

BASICALLY, IN A NUTSHELL

I don't think that I can remember the last time I ate a nut out of a shell. I have more than one nutcracker in my house, but I cannot recall the last time I purchased or ate a nut that wasn't already shelled for me. And, to think of it, I can't remember the last time I saw a nutshell. Yet, salespeople and other people presenting to me **CONSTANTLY** use this phrase.

The point here is not that nobody looks at the shells of nuts anymore, it's that it is maddening to me to hear salespeople, or anyone for that matter, using tired and meaningless cliché's like this one in their pitches.

It isn't just tired cliché's, its lazy words like "basically," "value-add," "total solution," and "value prop." If you want to be classified as a run of the mill salesperson, then use lots of these phrases. It indicates a tired pitch, a tired salesperson, and/or an un-exciting proposition.

Once again, nobody cares about your product. They care about their own problems, and how you can help them. Your prospects want to feel like you took the time to care about them and their problems. When you have a routine pitch littered with boring words, a prospect will feel like you are giving them your standard presentation instead of a customized one. You need to make prospects feel special. A generic presentation peppered with lazy words and tired clichés, is guaranteed to make the prospect feel like they are merely one in a herd. To make a prospect feel like they are your most important prospect and that you genuinely care about their problems, create a customized and energized presentation.

Did you take the time to understand their problems? How does your solution relate to what they do? Is your solution appropriate? Or are you just dialing a number, showing up for a meeting and playing the numbers game, hoping that enough people figure it out on their own for you to make quota.

You want to crush quota? Throw out the tired language and speak about your product in a compelling and direct way.

CLOSING TACTICS: GOOD TO GREAT

It's every salesperson's dream to become a great salesperson instead of just a good salesperson, and it's closing deals that make the difference, as I discussed above. When I first started writing this book, I noticed that the closing portion of the book was the smallest, yet the most critical element in becoming great, and the most important in the success of a start-up. I struggled for a while with what else to say about becoming great, and then I talked to several other sales people about how they became great, and we all agreed on one thing: *not asking for the close* was the single biggest obstacle to salespeople not becoming great. This means realizing it's time to ask for the order, asking for it, negotiating, and getting to a close.

When you dive into the details, you realize that the reason great salespeople have no issue with asking for the order is that they work all along in establishing the right relationship. These salespeople make sure that the prospects know they are being sold something and that a cash outcome is expected. They have been communicating the value, and most importantly, they are more concerned with solving the customer's pain, not about their own product.

Essentially, when you do the initial process correctly, you should have no problem in the final stages. The reason to buy will be clear and you with BOTH want it, even if your idea of how, how much, and when is different.

In this section, we will explore some interesting ways to push deals to the close. This part of the sale becomes considerably easier when all the other steps are done correctly.

ASK FOR THE ORDER

The single greatest obstacle to getting a sale, is not asking for it.

When you are sitting in front of a potential customer and you have to finally ask for the order, it can be terrifying. Why? When they say no, it's possible this is the end of the relationship or it's possible you will get the sale or learn more. The instinct of a greener salesperson is to make sure everything is perfect before finally asking them to buy. Yet, a more seasoned salesperson asks for the order quickly, in order to learn what it will take to actually get to the sale.

In many cases, I ask for the sale very early in the process. I want to hear, "well, we aren't quite ready to buy yet. We want to see how x, y, and z will happen, and of course, we would not buy until the next fiscal year." Wow! Think about how much I just learned by just asking for the order. Alternatively, I could have waited and wondered about why they weren't ready to buy. But now I know that I need x, y, and z.

If your prospect won't give you an answer about buying, what does that tell you? They may never buy – or they don't see the urgency. If you give them the product to use, or taking them out to lunch or golf, why would they upset that relationship? On the flip side, why are you buying them lunch if you can't get the sale. Just ask for it.

If asking for the sale scares them off, you weren't going to get the sale. It may be that you haven't done the initial value proposition correctly, but it may also be that they just don't want what you sell. You need to figure that out and if the problem is on your side, you now have the opportunity to fix it. If they were just stringing you along, well it's time to part ways – even if they are a very nice person.

Don't be afraid to ask for the order early and often.

IF I... WILL YOU

Whenever someone asks me about a particular negotiation point or tactic, I always tell him or her to remember the following phrase and to use it in every negotiation:

"If I.... will you..."

For example,

"If I drop the setup fee, will you be able to sign this week?"

"If I can get my boss to agree to the price reduction, will you agree to extend your contract from 12 months to 18 months?"

"If I commit to adding this feature in a future release, will you allow us to use your logo on our website?"

It's a simple idea of negotiation where you each get something, but I find thinking of always phrasing the question in this way, forces you to think about the negotiation process in the right way. And, it always reminds you to make sure that every time a prospect/customer asks you to give on something, they should know that they are also expected to give on something. That something may be as simple as giving you the order, or another non-cash item, but they are expected to give in order to get.

What you should never do, is give up something for nothing. When a customer asks for a feature, a reduction in price, a concession of any kind, they are trying to move the process forward (or stalling). This is your opportunity to also move the deal forward the way you want it to (or determine that this deal isn't real). If you always want to sell a win-win solution, then when your customer/prospect asks for something, you should be getting something for that, too.

Negotiations are rarely easy, but I find that remembering the simple "If I… will you," phrase keeps my brain in the right mode of thinking.

THE QUARTER IS ENDING

At the end of any quarter, if you are in sales, and if you are awake, you should be working on how to use the end of the quarter to get as many deals closed as possible.

Those weeks are key weeks to call all of your stalled deals and wake them up with an offer. This is the time to grab your April and May deals, and try to move them into Q1. This is the week to make sure the deals that you are counting on for Q1 actually happen.

Remember the "If I… will you" and call each and every deal that needs movement and use the end of Q1 as an excuse to reach out to them. Not to pester them, but to reach out to each and every deal in your pipeline no matter how far out and touch them.

Some resistance from salespeople I have managed on this:

- "But my customer told me not to call them until June." It doesn't matter. Call them now, and say, "I know you said don't call until June, but I just talked to my VP of Sales and he said that if you can close before the end of the month, I can offer you x. I thought the offer made a lot of sense and thought I'd reach out just in case." Your prospect, if nothing else, should appreciate that you thought of them. Make sure your offer is genuine and that you actually have something of value. Otherwise, you are killing the deal.

- "I left them a voicemail last week and they haven't called back." Again, it doesn't matter. Call them again and explain the offer. Leave another message and tell them you will send them an email as well. Or vice versa – send an email and then call and tell them you are following up on your email. Say, "I'm sorry if I'm being a pest, but I wanted to make sure you got the chance to hear about this offer that I'm being allowed to make if you sign before the end of the month."

- "I've already made them a sweetheart deal, and I don't have anything new to offer". Well, I certainly hope that you have already put an expiration date on a sweetheart deal, and if you haven't, then it is time to reach out and make sure that they know the deal expires at midnight on the last day of the quarter.

- "I'm afraid I will come off as pushy. " This is exactly the point. I always advocate win-win sales, and therefore, if you are calling just to hound them on where the deal is, then you WILL come off pushy. You should be calling with a genuine offer and with a genuine desire to get them as a customer at the best deal that you can offer. This is about applying a pressure point at the end of the quarter to potentially force a decision faster than they wanted to – and giving them an incentive for doing so.

When you need an edge or a reason to push a deal forward, the end of the quarter is a great time.

In many large companies, departments get "use-it or lose-it" budgets. What this means is that they get dollars for projects for that year, and if they don't use up all of that money by the end of the year, then they don't get to spend it. It does not roll over until the next year. Salespeople looking to finish out their own year great can capitalize on these budget realities. It requires you to be flexible in your pricing technique, but you can very often push through a sale that might otherwise take a very long time to close.

A manager at BigCo has $150,000 left in his budget for the rest of the year. He is evaluating your product for an initiative next year, and your product costs $400,000. Currently, in his mind, your product is completely on next year's budget. But, you ask about his unused budget and find out about the remaining amount. You determine with him the best way to bill him the $150,000 now, and the remaining $250,000 next year. If you can convince the manager to do this, not only do you secure a sale this year, you lock up your sale for next year, and leave the manager $150,000 extra on his budget for next year.

So, how do you flush out if there is an unused budget? Often it is as simple as asking. Managers may not even think of this as a possibility because it's never been proposed to them before. If they are not very forthcoming, and you really want to flush it out, you should continue to ask. One sweetener I have often used to get managers cozy with the idea is to offer them $1.10 credit for every dollar they spend with me today. So, if they handed me an invoice for $150,000, I would credit $165,000 off the cost of the project. This essentially makes the next year cost of my project an additional $15,000 less. Initial hesitation is often because they may not be sure that they want to use your product, or if what you suggest is okay with their company. But, most managers, knowing that they have money that will disappear and that this method will free up cash for next year's projects, will want to at least explore the offer. And if you have a manager willing to think outside the box, you will get the sale and an appreciative customer who will already know that you are the type of sales person in for the win-win.

Of course, you DO need to make sure that you aren't getting a manager into hot water, and I would never suggest something that circumvented corporate purchasing policies, but there are often creative ways to unbundle or unhook your product that makes it fit perfectly into this existing and disappearing budget money. Sometimes, the reason your product is scheduled for the following year is because it is part of some capital project that has dollars assigned to it. Once, I had a customer who had money left in his budget for professional services, but not for software. Yet I was trying to sell him software. Well, my software typically included installation services, training, first year support, and some data-loading services as part of the core product. All of those services were completely valid to be billed against his unused professional services budget. So, I unbundled these services for him, billed him in December for those items, and then billed him for the remaining software licenses in the next year. The tactic served the manager and me well. I got a sale and cash in the bank in the current year. He got to use this year's money for next year's project, and freed up more money in next year's budget (which I took too!). I also guaranteed that I was going to get a sale in the next year because by doing the first invoice, there was very little chance he would not take the second part.

As I've written before, you should be building relationships with your customers – not just selling them. This is actually one of those instances where what you are doing actually benefits everyone involved.

NEW YEAR, NEW TRY, NEW TACTIC

The start of every new sales period (be it quarter, year, or otherwise) can bring about positive and negative feelings for a salesperson. It's a clean slate and a new chance to crush it. But it also likely means you lost your accelerator that you were enjoying from crushing it last year, and now you have to start all over. You are on an even playing ground with other salespeople, when you were enjoying being on top. If you missed your mark last year, perhaps this is your chance to shine and make sure that you beat your numbers this year.

Regardless of how last year went for you as a salesperson, and assuming you haven't been sandbagging, you are going to struggle for a little bit to get your pipeline closing in the New Year. Your prospects are back fresh, they have their own year to plan out, they may have fresh budget but aren't as eager to spend it quickly.

So, what's a salesperson to do to make sure that the new sales period starts off great?

1. Find the companies that have a January 31 fiscal year end. You will be surprised how many companies have this in place. These are the companies that you will attack first to try the "end of the year run" technique. By using up their unused budgets that they may lose, you can set up a win-win for yourself. Don't be shy about asking for a contract that pays a portion in January and a portion in February. You get your goal, and they get to split the cost across two years. For private companies, you'll need to ask them about their fiscal year, but I've never had anyone refuse to give me that information when asked.

2. Go back to each prospect and every person who said no to you and give it another try. Situations change, and it's completely reasonable to **pick up the phone** and talk to those prospects to see if it's time to revisit, or if there is a better time to discuss this year. When you do call at the beginning of the year, it's a much softer call because you aren't calling them out of the blue. Most people receiving the call will understand that your quota has reset and may even expect the call. If you aren't pushy, but just trying to gauge whether or not the opportunity can be revived (money cleared up, their freeze is over, the competitive product they bought instead of yours is failing, etc.). Ask probing questions, but don't be pushy – just get back to the front of their minds – and see if any can shake out for a sale this year.

3. Revive the stalled deals. Everyone has deals that just stall in the pipeline. It frustrates sales managers (or any manager) to death that a deal is just sitting there, but I know that they happen. There are just those people that tell you they will buy, and then evade you, or frag you along, and you just aren't 100% sure when to mark them as a lost deal. The New Year is a great time to revisit and try to revive them. Often with a simple humorous call or email, I'm able to get a little traction on some deals. I've actually called people up and said, "Okay, so I failed at selling you last year, tell me what to do differently this

year." I've gotten some people to move at that point – with them actually feeling bad that they dragged me along last year and then working with me for a quicker close.

4. New tactic: It's a perfect time to try a new tactic with a prospect. For example, you might try a new package, or a new special. It won't seem as strange to offer something completely different to a stalled customer, because it's a new year and a fresh start.

The New Year is a great chance to get started on the right footing, and a great chance to try some new things.

NO CELEBRATING UNTIL THE DEAL IS SIGNED

In sales, it's very easy to start celebrating the minute a deal is closed. In fact, celebration often starts once the verbal commitment is given. But, if there is one thing that experience in sales will teach you, it is that you really can't celebrate until the contract is signed – and furthermore – you really can't celebrate until the cash is in the bank.

One month serves as a great case. It was an interesting one for two of my clients. For both of them, there were enough deals on the one-yard line that the odds seemed very likely that the goal would be hit. Yet so many of the deals got pushed into the next month that both missed the mark. It's worth noting that nearly all the deals are still in play. All that failed was creating enough urgency that the deals were able to close at the end of the month.

In at least half of the instances, the objectives were very clearly outlined.

"Fred, **if I give you this deal, will you** get us a signature before the end of the month?"

"Mark, I can certainly have this done before the end of the month and really want to."

"Great, so is there anything that would stop this getting signed and implemented?"

"No, Mark. I've read the contract and it all looks great. I'm bringing it in for signature tomorrow."

177

"Thanks Fred, looking forward to doing business with you."

Then…. total silence. No return phone calls, no indication of good or bad, no contract.

So what happened? Well, clearly there was an obstacle/objection that was not known, and the urgency that was created wasn't enough to move the needle. Perhaps it wasn't a fault of not asking – perhaps it was something that came up afterwards. Either way, it shows that even when your prospect tells you without a doubt that they will buy, and that the deal is done, it's not done until the ink is on the paper and the cash is in the bank.

For the most part, I believe the failure was in creating urgency to buy now. End of the quarter is something that people understand and expect, and "end of month" pushes did not resonate as well. For both clients, there were a lot of additional triggers that could have be used, and in the next month it was more clear to use those triggers to help get people to move rather than to just rely on "making our monthly number."

In your own sales efforts, you need to find those things that will get people to want to close now rather than later. Perhaps it is the lost revenue opportunity, cost savings opportunity, the summer sales rush, free upgrade promotion, or something else. The key to getting those deals across the finish line quickly will be that specific urgency goal.

It's okay to enjoy a verbal commitment with a smile, but unless you've found the urgency and reason to buy now, it's not a done deal. In fact it is never a done deal until ink is on paper and case is in the bank. So, just make sure that you don't ring that gong too early.

Someone asked me at a talk I gave about what I thought were the top five lessons for any new sales rep at a start-up. While every lesson in this book is important, if you can grasp the five below, you will be miles ahead of most.

1. **Nobody cares about your product.** Prospects care about their own problems, not your product. The faster you find their problem ("their pain") that you solve through your product, then the faster you will get to the sale. Selling the value of what you provide instead of the actual item you sell will get you further.

2. **Embrace the word "NO."** Don't be afraid to ask for the deal. Typical new salespeople let deals fester because they are afraid of hearing the word no. I say, get to the no. You will find the real reason for any objection – and eventually turn it into a yes through negotiation.

3) **Don't worry about money.** The salesperson who is constantly thinking about money will lose more deals than they win. Worry about finding the right solution for your prospects, and the money will follow.

4) **Listen.** God gave you two ears and one mouth so use them in that ratio. Listen twice as much as you speak and your prospect will tell you how to close the deal.

5) **There are no lost deals, only deals that didn't close now.** If you take a deal that you lose, and ruin it, you will **never** get that deal. Remember that your prospects may buy in the future or move to different companies and eventually buy. Treat the people at lost deals with the same respect that you treat closed deals, even if they pick your competitor. You never know when you may run into them again.

Good luck selling!

ACKNOWLEDGEMENTS

There are tons of influences in my life, but the ones that I truly believe made a difference in the production of this book: My parents Rich and Patricia who sacrificed too much to make sure I got all the opportunities they didn't, my wife Theresa for indulging my risky nature, my kids Erin, James, and Tina for providing me sufficient incentive to make everything successful, Danny Turano for being my loyal sales mentor and friend for the past decade, Mrs. Murphy and Mrs. Portas for seeing the best in me at a young age and putting me on step one of my path, Jim Walls for providing me my first amazing opportunity which pointed me on the path of entrepreneurship, Dr. Kevin Donahue for telling me I was the worst writer and later telling me I was the best writer in high school, David S. Rose for giving me access to the world, Evan Bartlett and Ryan Pipkin for pushing me to start writing a blog on sales which gave me my voice, the direct reports that helped my craft, especially Lauren "shoes and purses" Gearhart, all the clients of QuotaCrush who provided me the good and bad stories that I share in this book, and allowing other start-ups to learn from their failures and their triumphs, to Stevens Institute of Technology for providing the best education foundation for both problem solving and entrepreneurship, for the Hugh O'Brian Youth Foundation that gave me confidence and moxie to believe I was world-class before I knew it, to the investors who took chances on me, to Allison Riney for editing my book, and to all the countless other friends and members of my family who have had such a dramatic impact on my life. This book would not have been possible without all of the influences on my life, as this book is a reflection of my experiences, my career, and my ambition to be the person that my influences and I want me to be.

Printed in Great Britain
by Amazon